Trudy,

Will see you at the Table!

Jim

2-29-08
Ottawa

Such a pleasure to meet you and
talk with you. I know you will
always do well in our profession.

Best of Luck.

Jim

More Praise for
Why Should the Boss Listen to You?

"Jim Lukaszewski has personally helped resolve more corporate crises than anyone I know of. His experience 'in the trenches' equals the high quality of his judgment."

—Chester Burger, American Public Relations Leader Emeritus and PRSA Gold Anvil Winner

"This book is all muscle. It will challenge even the most trusted advisors to improve their skills. Hats off to Jim Lukaszewski for an actionable playbook and a good read."

—Lynn Casey, chief executive officer, Padilla Speer Beardsley

"I have both worked with Jim and learned from him. With his experience, intelligence, and grit he says what the client needs to hear, in the way it needs to be heard. Reading this book provides valuable insights and guidance to help you navigate the often treacherous waters swirling around management."

—Douglas Cooper, co-managing partner, Ruskin Moscou Faltischek, P.C.

"Lukaszewski, a brilliant strategic advisor, gives the secrets that can mean success for you."

—Robert L. Dilenschneider, author, *Power and Influence: The Rules Have Changed*

"If you want to be in your organization's inner circle and if you want to stay there, this book is a must-read. Jim Lukaszewski is hands down one of the brightest business strategists on the scene today. This is the handbook to your career success."

—Bob Frause, chairman and CEO, Frause, Seattle

"Jim Lukaszewski is a master at both giving advice to leaders and coaching others to become trusted advisors. This book provides valuable tools and techniques to help enhance anyone's advisory skills, and to help earn the trust and confidence of those at the top."

—Helio Fred Garcia, executive director, Logos Institute for Crisis Management and Executive Leadership, and adjunct professor of management, New York University

"Jim Lukaszewski is widely regarded as one of the country's preeminent authorities in crisis communications and issues management. What I admire most is Jim's innate desire to teach others. Through his professional practice and his writings, Jim relentlessly challenges us to elevate our thinking and our skills in order to drive strategic thinking throughout our respective organizations."

—Karen Muldoon Geus, former vice president, communications, The Children's Hospital of Philadelphia and Primestar Partners

"Jim Lukaszewski is the best strategic thinker I know. But what makes him even more valuable to clients is his ability to sell his recommendations to CEOs and senior management. That combination of talents is exceedingly rare."

—Robert E. Gorman, Robert E. Gorman Communication

"I've been a communication consultant to all types of organizations for more than thirty years, and I thought I knew all there was to know about offering advice to my clients—until I read Jim Lukaszewski's book. What a treasure trove of insights, experiences, and practical advice on how to become and remain a valued advisor. Read it and learn."

—Carole M. Gorney, director, Center for Crisis Public Relations and Litigation Studies, Lehigh University

"When your company is faced with a dire situation, there is great comfort in picking up the phone and hearing Jim Lukaszewski's voice. When we get in a tight spot, we rely on his wisdom and advice."

—Deborah L. Grant, vice president, university communications, Tulane University

"In *Why Should the Boss Listen to You?* Jim Lukaszewski draws on his long and successful career as a counselor to senior management in a clear and straightforward way. No matter what your profession, the Disciplines will help you see higher and further."

—Stephanie Harwood, S. M. Harwood Consulting

"One of the most 'trusted strategic advisors' I know is Jim Lukaszewski. If you want your boss to listen to you, read this book—and everything else Jim writes."

—Richard Jernstedt, chief marketing officer, executive vice president, senior partner, Fleishman-Hillard

"In this book the magician reveals his secrets. Guess what? Some of it *is* magic, but most of it is integrity in action. You can do it, too."

—George Kroloff, George Kroloff & Associates

"Jim's diverse background, depth of experience, and hands-on battle skills in the trenches deliver superior results; his strategic advice and counsel made the difference."

—Seth Kursman, vice president, government affairs and communications, AbitibiBowater Inc., Montreal

"As the CEO of my own firm today, and as Jim's mentor and college advisor years ago, I am reminded of the depth of perspective Jim has always displayed in operating as a trusted advisor to so many, even as he completed his education. This book will open up his wise and inventive approaches to guiding and advising to a much wider business audience. I encourage you to read this book and be inspired by it."

—Judith Pendergrass, chief executive officer, Martin McAllister, Consulting Psychologists, Inc.

"Jim is well known for helping those in the C-suite deal with crises. With his new book, *Why Should the Boss Listen to You?* he teaches us how to build the kind of trusting relationship needed to be the first person the CEO calls when there's a situation brewing—or when he or she just wants to hear some straight talk."

—Mela Sera, account supervisor, IMRE Communications

"Jim's ability to quickly assess issues and offer pragmatic solutions in a clear, understandable fashion makes him a valuable partner in running a business in these fast and turbulent times. Many of my line managers still comment on how his counsel helped them, and how they use his tenets of communication every day."

—Robert M. Sherwood, division human resources lead, Flavours, Givaudan Schweiz AG

"Jim Lukaszewski is a premier counselor to CEOs for one simple reason: he knows how they think, what matters to them—and what does not matter to them. Too many who contend for influence in the executive suite attempt to impose their notions of what the boss should know about their functional area. Far better that they put themselves in the boss's shoes and bring useful insight that helps the leader move the organization forward. Jim's book shows aspiring counselors exactly how to do this."

—David J. Therkelsen, executive director, Crisis Connection

"Jim often is at the table with spot-on counsel and laser-focused strategy that CEOs and other experts and advisors can quickly embrace, and an intensity that makes the difference in the final outcome."

—Marilyn Waters, director of media relations, Fortune 100 Company

"Every senior leader worth his or her salt should listen to what Jim Lukaszewski has to say. Often it has been Jim's unique experience, insight, and counsel that made the difference between success and failure for leaders facing the most challenging problems and issues of their careers."

—Richard J. White, vice president, corporate communications, Wisconsin Energy Corporation / We Energies

Why Should the Boss Listen to You?

The Seven Disciplines of the Trusted Strategic Advisor

James E. Lukaszewski

JOSSEY-BASS
A Wiley Imprint
www.josseybass.com

Published by Jossey-Bass
A Wiley Imprint
989 Market Street, San Francisco, CA 94103-1741—www.josseybass.com

Jossey-Bass books and products are available through most bookstores. To contact Jossey-Bass
directly call our Customer Care Department within the U.S. at 800-956-7739, outside the
U.S. at 317-572-3986, or fax 317-572-4002.

Jossey-Bass also publishes its books in a variety of electronic formats. Some content that
appears in print may not be available in electronic books.

Library of Congress Cataloging-in-Publication Data

Lukaszewski, James E.
      Why should the boss listen to you? : the seven disciplines of the trusted strategic advisor /
James E. Lukaszewski. — 1st ed.
         p.   cm.
      Includes index.
      ISBN-13: 978-0-7879-9618-5 (cloth)
         1. Business consultants.   2. Leadership.   3. Decision making.   4. Management.   I. Title.
HD69.C6L855   2008
650.1'3—dc22

                                                                                      2007029342

Printed in the United States of America
FIRST EDITION
HB *Printing*   10 9 8 7 6 5 4 3 2 1

Contents

Managers and leaders trust those who show interest in and are
knowledgeable about operations and the work of leaders. To be
a management advisor, you need to be able to talk more about
your boss's goals and objectives than about whatever your staff
function happens to be. You need to be able to see the business
or organization operationally and through the leader's eyes.

Leadership is always about strategy. This chapter discusses the
concepts and ideas behind being strategic, including the seven
virtues of a strategist, the four phases of strategic thinking,
and five fatal strategic flaws. Find out how much of a strategist
you are.

The advisor who can forecast tomorrow with almost any level of
accuracy will be invited back time and time again. One of the
great insights into being a powerful forecaster is understanding
how to learn from the patterns of past experiences. This chapter
offers the five lessons of scenario pattern awareness and examples
of the insights patterns can reveal.

Giving advice is an art that starts where the boss is and where
he or she has to go. This chapter will teach you how to structure
your advice to ensure that you are clearly understood and that
the boss can act on what you are advising. It also offers pitfalls
to giving advice, some strategies and techniques to help you
structure advice, and three strategic tools to use.

One of the skills that management schools fail to teach is how
to take advice from those whose advice one seeks. To see your
ideas come alive, teach the boss how to take and to use your
advice. You may be surprised at how receptive your boss will be.

This chapter offers four elements of constructive advice, seven approaches to providing effective advice, and a way to assess your daily effectiveness.

The fundamental premise of this book is that you are the table whenever you are in the presence of those you are advising, even if you are the only one in the room with them. Forget searching for this mythical place, located somewhere in the vicinity of the boss's office. Understand the leaders' environment and thinking. Develop the disciplined approach this book offers, and the table will be full whenever you are there. This confident attitude, coupled with sensible, useful, and constructive advice, is what the boss expects, relies on, and respects you for in the process.

On becoming the number one Number Two:

To all the Number Twos and those who want to be more significant trusted advisors—the disappointed, frustrated, yet eager and persistent staff people in communications, corporate strategy, finance, human resources, law, IT, business continuation and recovery, compliance, and security who know that if only they could get to the inner circle and be heard, their advice could save the day and avoid career-defining moments for their boss.

This book will help you become the number one Number Two you imagine yourself to be, wherever you work, whether you are an internal expert or an outside consultant. The concepts talked about here will make your professional life richer, more professionally rewarding, and exhilarating.

Working at the top is exciting, intense, and often fraught with confrontation and the clash of big egos and ideas. Some days it is like being in intellectual combat. Winston Churchill once remarked that there is absolutely nothing more invigorating than being shot at, and missed.

Welcome to the line of fire.

Preface

Why did you pick up this book? Let me guess: you are in finance, accounting, human resources, law, public relations, marketing, security, IT, compliance, strategic planning, or midlevel operations, and you are not being heard. You want to be, but you cannot be heard. You need to find some way to be noticed, or they hear you but ignore you, or someone is blocking your way to influencing events and individuals. The greatest frustration of all, especially for individuals aspiring to be influential, is not being invited to important meetings or being invited in too late. By the time you do get called in, become aware of what is going on, or are permitted to participate, all the expensive outside consultants, attorneys, and assorted advice givers have staked out the avenues you might have successfully recommended. Employees in every staff function feel this way and suffer from this problem; so do a lot of midlevel operations managers. Individuals from each group feel the strong need to be heard; they are paid to be heard.

This is a book about gaining influence and becoming a key advisor, about getting to where you can truly be heard, whether you work inside as an expert or outside as a consultant.

Advisor to whom? What do I mean by "the boss"? Even if your boss or manager is low in the organizational structure, this book can be of great benefit to you. The qualities that the CEO's advisor needs are similar to those needed by anyone, at any level, who serves as an advisor to another individual or group of individuals. The thinking, habits, disciplines, and attitudes are very much the same.

Having influence means being remembered, being asked in on decisions and strategy well before the strategies are selected and the decisions need to be made. It is creating the desire in someone else to hear your views before he or she makes important decisions or takes actions that matter.

One of the realities of wanting influence is that there is only so much face time, airtime, meeting time, and thinking time available to those who run organizations. The closer you get to the top, the fewer in number there are of these important people. Therefore, to begin having influence requires a personal strategy of accomplishment, commitment, and personal incremental progress that helps set you apart from the wannabes, the dreamers, and the self-servers. This differentiation needs to start wherever you are in your organization today and to continue until you get to the level you seek to achieve. You will need a strategy to be noticed. This is why I wrote *Why Should the Boss Listen to You? The Seven Disciplines of the Trusted Strategic Advisor.*

Ask yourself two serious, honest questions: What will my boss learn or do better if he or she listens to me? What do I gain if the boss does listen?

When I ask these questions of other advisors, the usual reasons I hear are, "I have a more specialized knowledge of the business," "My ideas are certainly as good as anyone else's," "How will I ever progress if my current boss keeps blocking my best ideas from getting to the top?" "I am better than those already in place," and my all-time favorite, "I have the right to be heard." If you have or hear other reasons why the boss should listen to you, write them down. You can try validating them as you learn more about what it takes to become a trusted strategic advisor, at whatever level you happen to be working.

Now ask the same questions from the boss's point of view. The responses I hear quite often relate to past mistakes and judgments, such as "They would not have made that agonizing retrenchment decision if they had listened to me." "If I had been in the meeting, our approach to that opportunity would have been entirely different and far more successful, and we would have kept more of the business." "Had they asked me, we could have avoided that dumb series of mistakes." "The boss has blind spots and deficiencies." The mind-set these comments reveal is quite common, but as you will discover, this sort of approach will always get in the way of your becoming a trusted advisor.

Here is a test of your current level of influence in your organization:

- Do people hold up meetings, waiting for you to arrive to make important contributions or interpretations of current events?
- Do people remember what you say and perhaps quote you in other places and venues?
- Do people tell your stories and share your lessons as though those stories belonged to them?
- Do people learn things from you that they acknowledge to you and remark about to others?
- Do others seek out your opinion and ideas or share their agendas and beliefs with you in the hope of influencing you to influence the behavior of others more senior than you?

Even if you aced this test, this book will help you.

For more than thirty years, I have coached and counseled the men and women who run very large corporations and organizations—helping them deal with tough, touchy, sensitive corporate management communications issues, often when their leadership of the organization is at stake. I have advised top executives facing issues ranging from media-initiated investigations to product recalls and plant closings, from ethics failures and criminal litigation to corporate takeovers and serious executive malfeasance. As an individual trusted with some of the most personal and important information my clients have, I am constantly putting myself in their shoes, looking at the world from their perspective, and helping them adjust to current realities; compensate for issues and problems that were probably self-generated; identify threats, vulnerabilities, and opportunities; and be constructively motivated to move successfully into the future. My job is always to assist these individuals and those on whom they rely to recognize the nature of the times and adapt effectively so that they can continue running organizations with championship, leadership, compassion, and accountability.

Over the years, I have learned a lot of lessons about working with CEOs, boards, and senior executives, and I share them in this book. My goal is to help internal advisors, outside consultants, and the leaders they counsel reach new levels of effectiveness and success by gaining a much deeper understanding of their relationship to each other and to the mutual goals they have yet to achieve together.

What This Book Offers

Why Should the Boss Listen to You? The Seven Disciplines of the Trusted Strategic Advisor provides advice and techniques that apply to all internal staff functions (finance, accounting, human resources, law, public relations, marketing, security, IT, and strategic planning) and to outside consultants in these functional staff areas. It provides systematic, pragmatic, and sensible ingredients and processes for getting to and working at the highest levels and having maximum impact as a trusted advisor. If being in the inner circle is a bit premature for you, these are techniques for you to learn that will help you earn or build your way into these select groups of influential individuals.

This book will help you develop the skills you need to become a trusted advisor who is sought out and called in earlier—while you still have the ability to influence decisions and have an impact. It is critical to this endeavor that you know how CEOs and other top executives think, understand what matters to them and how they operate, and clearly know what they expect and need from you as their advisor—and I offer my perspective on all these topics.

You will learn how CEOs perceive those who hold staff functions, and learn about the behaviors and attitudes of staff that hold them back—making them less influential than they could be. You will discover specific skill sets you need to become a trusted strategic advisor, and receive guidance on developing those skills; you will also gain a better understanding of what is expected of you and how to meet those expectations.

To be more specific, in Part One of this book, you will learn:

- **How leaders think and operate.** There are many powerful realities that drive the world of today's CEOs. If you are serious about advising people at senior levels, you need to understand what they are trying to accomplish, what motivates them, the problems they face, how they think and make decisions, and, most important, how they achieve success.

- **How to think and operate in ways that meet the boss's expectations.** The trusted advisor acts to meet the leader's expectations, putting self-interest aside. Real leaders seek out many voices, and always prioritize the advice they receive. To be effective, the advisor must know how the boss measures the value of advice and ensure that his or her advice meets this standard.

- **How to achieve real impact.** Being listened to and having impact require that you gain the confidence of top leadership, understand and speak their language, avoid the typical staff shortcomings that annoy bosses, respect the boss's time, give useful feedback, and meet other expectations.

Part Two of the book presents the seven-discipline approach to becoming a trusted strategic advisor. Each chapter explains how you can develop one of the seven crucial disciplines on which the trusted advisor's success depends:

1. **Be trustworthy.** If you want to be an advisor at top levels, or at any level for that matter, you and those you advise must

maintain each other's trust. Being trustworthy is one of the foundation disciplines; it permits you to accomplish the rest of your objectives. The absence of trust means rejection.

2. **Become a verbal visionary.** Verbal skill is the main tool of leaders—speaking effectively, describing the future, giving instructions, and teaching others. People exercise leadership mostly through verbally expressed ideas, concepts, and stories. Many elements of successful advice giving and advising also demand excellent verbal skill. How are your verbal skills? This is a crucial discipline.

3. **Develop a management perspective.** Although it is certainly necessary to have an area of special expertise as a threshold requirement for becoming a trusted advisor, managers and leaders need counselors and coaches who can see the world from their perspective. Is the advice you give only from the perspective of your function, or can you truly see the world more as the manager or leader sees it?

4. **Think strategically.** Can you develop the mind of a strategist? Do you understand what strategy is, how it is applied, and why it is so essential to management and leadership success? This is the discipline of being intentionally different and intentionally memorable, seeing the world from unique and new perspectives, every time.

5. **Be a window to tomorrow: understand the power of patterns.** A crucial ingredient for successful advice giving is the ability to use your understanding of known patterns of events and circumstances to recognize or forecast the results of various actions and decisions. Are you a pattern analyst? Can you learn from your experiences or the experiences of others, then translate the key ingredients into lessons that leaders need to hear from you?

6. **Advise constructively.** Can you give advice and share your knowledge in ways that leaders and managers understand?

Can you channel your intuition and imagination in ways that make you understandable and your advice actionable, in an operational context?

7. **Show the boss how to use your advice.** This may be the most important discipline of all: teaching those you advise how to value, act on, and benefit from what you have to offer.

Whether you are reading this book from the perspective of years in your position as an important manager and organizational leader; as a first-time, frontline supervisor; or as someone fresh out of college full of ideas, energy, and fresh solutions, this book will help you become more effective and more influential, and have a more important and successful career.

Crucial Questions

As you move into the text of this book and begin absorbing the concepts it shares, there are other crucial questions you need to continuously ask yourself:

- Why do I want to be heard by my boss?
- Why should the boss listen to me about anything? What's in it for him or her?
- What is not working now? Why?
- There are clearly some risks if I do punch through and get heard by the boss; am I ready for those?
- Am I ready to begin being more brutally honest with myself?
- Can I train myself to focus on what really matters?
- How willing am I to change myself to have more influence?

My intention is to help you change your life by learning how to change the lives of others. It should happen chapter by chapter, concept by concept, and discipline by discipline. It is a fascinating journey, one from which, ultimately, you will benefit more than anyone else.

Good luck.

September 2008

James E. Lukaszewski
Snug Harbor
Danbury, Connecticut

Acknowledgments

This book came into being through a very fortuitous accident. I was in San Francisco visiting some of my colleagues at the International Association of Business Communicators (IABC)—Julie Freeman, Chris Grossgart, and Natasha Spring, now Natasha Nicholson. During the luncheon, we were talking about various projects, problems, and situations, and I was asked, "Why haven't you written more books?"

My rather hesitant response was that finding an agent was almost impossible and a publisher just about as difficult. Almost in unison they said they had connections with publishers and could put me together with one. The next day Kathe Sweeney, an acquisitions editor at Jossey-Bass in San Francisco, contacted me. I submitted a proposal electronically following that conversation. Within seven days I had an offer from this publisher. This is what I call having connections.

Through Kathe, I met (virtually) a developmental editor, Alan Schrader. His guidance and suggestions were crucial to getting the book done. Alan caused three amazing things to happen. First, he cracked the code for me about how I should present the contents. Next, he suggested an ingenious approach to the Table of Contents, and worked to keep my voice, the voice of the book.

So it is true that it takes a village to write a book. In this case, there are many others who took the time to review the manuscript or to make helpful observations based on their knowledge of my work.

The list of these wonderful people begins with James M. Alexander, my youngest son, who was quoted in the *Wall Street*

Journal and many other business publications before his father, started companies at an age younger than his father, and spent time on the manuscript and offered significant advice along the way, all the while completing his MBA at the University of Oxford.

Chester Burger, APR, Fellow PRSA, who is a career-long friend, advisor, mentor, and supporter, and the first to look at his profession from the perspective of being a business advisor rather than a staff communications person, offered amazing chapter-by-chapter commentary.

Lynn Casey, APR, chairman and CEO of Padilla Speer Beardsley Inc. in Minneapolis, Minnesota, whose career I have followed from the beginning, toughened up the text with her laserlike observations.

Douglas A. Cooper, Esq., a cool friend of many years and the managing partner in Long Island's second-largest law firm, is a spirited, intellectually active, and energizing mentor who helped my voice live in the text as the book progressed.

Mary Ann Cotton, APR, Boston, a former employee who taught me a lot along the way, allowed me to tell a number of stories about her in this book.

Robert L. Dilenschneider, chairman and CEO of the Dilenschneider Group Inc., is the author most recently of *Power and Influence: The Rules Have Changed.* His constructive short notes, comments, and compliments literally throughout my career have dramatically affected many of the ideas and concepts that I learned to use over the years and that appear in this book.

Robert Frause, APR, Fellow PRSA, whose Seattle-based consulting firm, the Frause Group, is always listed by *Washington CEO Magazine* as one of the "Best Companies to Work For," is my idol as a professional and a CEO.

Carol M. Gorney, APR, Fellow PRSA, a public relations professor at Lehigh University in Pennsylvania, consultant, and part-time resident of China advising the Chinese government, took time to work through the entire manuscript and thoroughly analyze and comment on it.

Deborah L. Grant, vice president of university communications at Tulane University, has inspired me for many years. Her amazing account of the rising floodwaters as Hurricane Katrina struck Tulane should be a book of its own one day.

Stephanie M. Harwood, APR, Harwood Consulting, one of the first people I met after moving from Minneapolis to New York, is a career-long friend and supporter who also spent an extraordinary amount of time working through the manuscript and making helpful suggestions from her perspective, despite being deeply engaged in the completion of her MBA thesis.

Richard Jernstedt, chief marketing officer, executive vice president, and senior partner of Fleishman-Hillard, Inc., is one of the great pragmatists and realists in public relations. Conversations with Rich are always meaningful and productive.

George Kroloff, a senior consultant based in the Washington, D.C., area and another career-long supporter, carefully reviewed the manuscript and made many, many truly insightful line-by-line comments.

Seth Kursman, vice president of communications and government affairs for AbitibiBowater Inc., is a young man whose career has taken him from the back roads of Ohio where he worked with angry neighbors to Stamford, Connecticut, then to Maine and Texas, where he handled ever more complex government relations problems, and then to Canada where he is a now a trusted strategic advisor engaged in international economic diplomacy.

Donald M. Levin, APR, Fellow PRSA, president of Levin Public Relations & Marketing, Inc., one of my great supporters from the moment I arrived in New York more than twenty years ago, and who has often taken my work more seriously than I have, closely examined the text and made substantive comments.

Charles T. Lukaszewski, my oldest son, who was published in *Vital Speeches of the Day* while in high school, coauthored a commercial book, and also started businesses at far younger ages than his father, provided the most significant and penetrating commentary as the manuscript progressed.

Helen I. Ostrowski, APR, Fellow PRSA, global CEO of Porter Novelli, has been a touchstone for me on many issues and someone whose experience helps her and those she counsels look at questions and ideas from very interesting new perspectives.

Judith A. Pendergrass, Ph.D., CEO and owner of Martin-McAllister Consulting, a human resources consulting firm based in Minneapolis, Minnesota, was my college advisor and one of three people responsible for my being where I am today. She did an extraordinarily thorough job of reviewing the manuscript and making many important suggestions and comments.

Tim Ring, CEO of C. R. Bard, Inc., in New Providence, New Jersey, made comments that were especially helpful, as they were based on the variety of very senior staff positions he has held, including being the senior vice president for human resources, prior to becoming CEO.

Mela Sera, APR, is a bright young rising public relations star about whom you will be hearing more as her career progresses.

David J. Therkelsen, APR, Fellow PRSA, executive director of Crisis Connection in Minneapolis, is a lifelong friend and another CEO who rose through the ranks of staff capacities to get there. He added crucial insights and reality checks as a senior executive recipient of consultant advice.

Robert W. Turner, now senior vice president of corporate relations with Union Pacific Railroad in Omaha, Nebraska, one of my first major East Coast clients and a consumer of my advice for more than twenty years, provided his usual witty, insightful, and pragmatic observations.

Richard J. White, vice president of corporate communications, the senior staff executive at We Energies (Wisconsin Electric Power Company), and a highly trusted advisor himself, helped me look at the world from his corporate vantage point of many years.

Davis Young, APR, Fellow PRSA, is a professional colleague of more than twenty years and fellow agency chief executive, who in recent years became an enthusiastic cheerleader for people like me. An author, teacher, and trusted advisor in his own right, Davis helped pull the more sophisticated concepts together and make them more usable.

William M. Hart, partner in the New York office of Proskauer Rose LLP, provided help on two crucial levels. He decoded the labyrinth of book publishing contracting and guided me with a combination of calmness and determination.

Kerrigan C. West, my associate now for many years, whose encyclopedic knowledge of what is in my brain and in the computer was essential. She knows what I have published and where I have been quoted, and played a crucial role in keeping this project focused, removing extraneous and distracting material, keeping my ideas consistent with past publications, and recognizing where intentional shifts in thinking have occurred—all of this while managing her primary responsibility, assisting me in my client consulting practice and professional activities.

Barbara Bray Lukaszewski, my wife of forty-four years and the mother of our two boys, has been my pal, friend, confidante, and anchor of sanity since we were children. On top of that, we have spent the last thirty years in business together. It's her smiley face every morning and her enthusiastic, productive, and completely focused participation in everything I do that is responsible for who I am and whatever I have accomplished in my lifetime.

My profound thanks to all of you. Any mistakes, problems, or errors that may have slipped through this gauntlet of helpful, well-meaning friends and colleagues are mine, and mine alone.

About the Author

James E. Lukaszewski (loo-ka-SHEV-skee) has been a trusted strategic advisor for most of his career, both during his service in government and later as he became a communications management consultant. He advises, coaches, and counsels the men and women who run very large corporations and organizations. His work as founder, CEO, and chairman of the Lukaszewski Group, Inc., is managing and counteracting tough, touchy, sensitive corporate communications issues. His broad-based experience ranges from media-initiated investigations to product recalls and plant closings, from criminal litigation to takeovers. The situations he helps resolve often involve conflict, controversy, community action, activist opposition, and civil or criminal litigation.

Jim has the unique ability to help executives look at problems from a variety of principled perspectives. He has personally counseled, coached, and guided thousands of executives in organizations large and small from many cultures. He is one of the few who can and truly does coach CEOs.

His name appeared in *Corporate Legal Times* as one of "28 Experts to Call When All Hell Breaks Loose" and in *PR Week* as one of twenty-two "crunch-time counselors who should be on the speed dial in a crisis."

Jim is the author of five previous books. *Influencing Public Attitudes: Strategies That Reduce the Media's Power* remains a classic work in the field of direct communication. The Public Relations Society of America published his four-volume *Executive Action Crisis Communication Management System: War Stories and Crisis*

Communication Strategies, an Anthology; Crisis Communication Planning Strategies, a Workbook; Crisis Communication Plan Components and Models: Crisis Communication Management Readiness; and *Media Relations During Emergencies, a Guide*. He has published twenty-five monographs and hundreds of articles on critical communication subjects.

His Web site, www.e911.com, created in 1998, is considered a global reference for those who advise leaders in all areas of business, government, and the nonprofit sector when trouble occurs.

Introduction

Leaders and Their Advisors

This book had its genesis several years ago on a bitterly cold winter day. Late on a Friday afternoon, I received a call from the president of a huge aluminum processing company. He was in the middle of labor talks, and things were going badly. In addition, he had just learned from his manager of health and safety that the Natural Resource Defense Council (NRDC) had publicly announced that day in Washington that his plant was a national target for reduction of excessive aluminum oxide emissions. (Aluminum oxide, at that time, was on the U.S. Environmental Protection Agency's list of toxic substances. It has since been delisted.)

On top of this, the union and the NRDC had apparently formed a team to bring pressure on the company from different directions. The CEO's general counsel had found me through a colleague suffering a similar fate.

The CEO wanted me to arrive on Sunday night so that I could spend some time with the senior management team before all hell broke loose. He mentioned that his director of corporate communications (whom I will call Susan) would meet me at the airport Sunday night.

As I came off the plane there was a young (younger than me) woman standing there examining each passenger as he or she walked by (this was well before the security imposed by 9/11). When she called out a version of my name, I realized that it was Susan and introduced myself. She told me to follow her to the baggage claim area. I sensed a little tension. I was taking up her personal family time, coming in Sunday evening, somewhat late.

My bags arrived, and as we walked to her car, I asked a couple of perfunctory questions about the weather and how things were going. She remained really quiet. As we put the luggage in the trunk, she said, "The boss only told me yesterday that you were coming in." Not a good start, but I mentioned that the boss and I had talked a couple of times during the week and that he had only invited me late Friday afternoon.

As she started the engine, Susan mentioned that for my departure there would be a cab or car service to get me back to the airport. As we got on the highway heading toward town, I said, "Why don't I tell you about what I envision happening in the next day or two, so we can make some plans?" She grunted, which I took to mean okay, and I began to outline what I saw the various meetings and activities to be, how we would start very early and rumble on through the day.

After I had been talking for a few minutes, she looked at me and essentially exploded. "I've been here nine years—nine long, hard years. I've learned a lot, I know a lot, I help these people every day, and still they call in someone like you," she said. "I've worked with consultants most of my career here and even before I came here. You all make little messes in different places that I have to clean up or live with after you are gone, and even with all the access people like you get to the CEO and other important people, they still wind up coming to me and taking my advice. But most of you do more damage than you realize and much more long-term harm to me and my communications program and what we're trying to accomplish here with very limited resources." She also indicated that she felt a little betrayed by her boss because he only mentioned inviting me when he told her to pick me up at the airport.

By the time she finished airing her complaints, we were at the hotel. My final comment to her was that there were going to be a number of meetings that I would attend but to which she would not be allowed. I told her that I would do my best to get her into those meetings. Whatever transpired in those meetings I would share with her fully, and I'd make sure that she was as much in the loop as she could be. She nodded and left.

The next day, we passed each other several times. As it turned out, we were in most meetings together, but there were several that were just for operating people and me. She and I chatted a couple times about things we were learning, and I briefed her on those meetings I had attended without her.

The second morning, the last day of my visit, we crossed paths, and Susan rather cheerily said, "I'm going to be taking you to the airport this afternoon myself." This was probably a good sign. I wondered what had changed.

As we packed up and started for the airport, I asked her why she had decided to drive me there. She said, "I've been watching you very carefully for these two days, trying to figure out why they call people like you when I'm here. I've paid my dues, and it seems to me that we give almost identical advice."

"What did you learn?" I asked. She responded by saying that she had observed some things that made her think a lot more carefully about how she does her own work. I asked for an example.

She talked about how I handled highly charged topics in large groups. She mentioned that her style, when she wanted to make a point, was to push as hard as she possibly could. "It doesn't seem to go so well, very often," she said. "They like my ideas when the news is good, but they become hard of hearing when the news isn't so good. But you have a way of telling stories or giving examples that tend to blunt people's feelings or emotions, so they let you continue talking, and they listen. Many are writing while you are speaking. You have the habit that when attacked by one individual, you turn your back, and then, talking to someone else, you respond to the person who had attacked you or your idea, but to someone else. That was a very interesting technique."

"Why?" I asked.

"Because it worked."

So I asked her, "What did you learn from that?"

She said, "I need to think less about achieving the point I'm trying to make and see if I can't find other ways to stay in the conversation that are meaningful to everyone in the room. I'd like them to write down what I say . . ."

"What else did you learn?"

She said, "You tend to use small numbers a lot when you talk—two, three, and four, mostly. I know this is intended to focus discussion, and it seems to get things moving. I thought that was a very helpful technique and something I could do if I thought about it."

"Of course you can," I said, "and of course you should. Using small numbers like that is very powerful, and does keep people better focused on what we are trying to accomplish. It is how I force them, sometimes almost against their will, to write things down. What else did you learn?"

"The biggest thing is the stories. You seem to have a story for everything. It sounds as though you've worked in every industry, worked on every kind of problem imaginable, and you have all these lessons to share through stories. This is my biggest problem. I've only really worked here. I don't get out like you do, to see a lot of things and have the ability to collect stories that might help me give more powerful advice."

"Do you belong to any professional communicator associations, or organizations for HR people or administrators?" I asked. She said she did and talked about a couple of them. I suggested that because she probably had a lot of vacation time built up (which she immediately agreed she did), she should take occasional days off to visit her colleagues and take a look at what was happening in those businesses, for the express purpose of developing or pulling together stories she could use in a variety of settings in her own work.

"Anything else you noticed that seemed important to you?" I asked.

"You do seem to be much more comfortable in the presence of our senior people than I often am. But I still think the advice I give is at least as good as yours, and ultimately that will be what people rely on."

I asked, "Do you think it's important that we give the same advice?" She said she thought so because too many distractions and different ideas would interfere with solving problems.

My response was that if I am successful, typically I can make one, two, or at the most three things happen that are significant in terms of moving the process forward and finding solutions or answers. And in most cases, those solutions, answers, or insights rely on existing internal processes and people for execution, as well as those executives and, usually, the boss, who take on the advice as their own.

I then asked if she knew or could guess why the boss had called in someone like me, as well as a variety of other outside voices that she had not expected, without telling her and lots of others either. "Yes," she said. "He's afraid, and his job may well be on the line if things really go badly here. He wants to be sure that he covers all his bases and is making the best decisions possible. And he wants a broader range of options to choose from. As much as I hate it, I know he needs to go beyond the advice and advisors he has every day to feel confident."

"This may be the biggest lesson from your visit," she said. "Our job is to provide a suitable menu of alternatives from which the CEO will select the ingredients for solutions and actions."

"That's right; it's never about the advisor," I said. "He's facing at least one career-defining moment. And one is all it takes. He's getting all of his advisors aligned, organized, and ready to work before his struggle begins. The goal is to have a variety of ideas to choose from rather than one locked-up approach that he's stuck with."

As we neared the airport, I told her that one of the things I admired about her boss was his ability to actually accept, absorb, and apparently apply the advice he was getting. This was a major weakness in many executives with whom I have worked, especially when there is serious trouble.

I also told her that at every opportunity, the boss and other senior executives had praised her and said they could rely on her thinking and advice. Clearly, she was highly regarded.

The lessons Susan learned are powerful for every advisor who wants to be trusted and wants to play at a strategic level. Her story illustrates the transition even experienced pros need to make to become more effective advisors to senior leaders. This kind of work really requires putting yourself in the other person's shoes, looking at the world from his or her perspective, and letting that approach dominate how you think, how you speak, how you coach, and how you contribute. It also means recognizing that the boss is rarely looking for advisor consensus or that single big idea, but rather good solid insight, options, and even conflicting views for his or her own decision making. Executives execute based on the choices at hand, especially when the clock is close to running out.

Susan remains a colleague to this day.

Professional Potholes

Some aspects of this work are so obvious that they often are overlooked and become professional potholes. The first is that every organization, whether it is for profit, not for profit, government, or military, can be divided into two parts: staff and operations. And, of course, operations is where the business is done and run. It is where the products are sold or manufactured, where the services are provided, that sort of thing. Wherever the business or organization is generating revenue, that is the operating side of the business.

Operators run the business organization; staff functions exist to help these operators do a better job, every day. The staff side of the business essentially comprises public relations, human resources, law, finance, security, government relations, IT, strategic planning, regulatory affairs, marketing, and other service functions. Staff functions are expenses against revenue. In other words, staff are always on the cost side of the business ledger. Staff often spend a lot of time debating their bottom-line value. To most operating executives, this line of thinking is a waste of time, although operators are often greatly amused by the lengths that staff will go to justify their existence and ideas. The more that staff try to justify their existence based on their contribution to the bottom line, the more intensively the CEO and other senior operating executives subject staff expenses to scrutiny and measurability. If you are intent on basing your staff value case on your bottom-line contribution, you are likely to be working alone and worrying a lot.

The premise behind being a trusted strategic advisor is that you bring extraordinary value to your relationship with executives, well beyond the cost impact of your advice. Most staff people make the mistake of assuming that if they are in the presence of senior leadership from time to time, they are automatically looked at as at least an occasional member of the inner circle. This is what I call the face-time fantasy. Actually, you know in your heart and in your guts that it's a fantasy. The boss may know the names of your grandchildren or your kids, where you vacation, where your wife or husband was born, where you went to school, or your golf score, but almost none of this has anything to do with running the business. Your job, as you will learn throughout this book, is to make certain that the time you spend with executives is limited, focused, and overwhelmingly in their operational interest. We will delve more deeply into this in the discipline sections. Right from the beginning, take a breath and lose the self-imposed false impression that the more time you get to spend with the boss in a variety of settings, the more likely it is that he or she will turn to you for advice.

Five Imperatives for the Trusted Strategic Advisor

Any staff person—or any consultant—needs to do five key things to become a trusted advisor to senior leaders:

1. Jettison staff-based assumptions.
2. See the whole board.

3. Tolerate constructive ambiguity, but strive for certainty.

4. Maximize your prerogatives.

5. Develop real expertise beyond your staff function.

Let us examine each of these imperatives.

Jettison Staff-Based Assumptions

One of the most profound underlying concepts this book is designed to convey to you is the imperative to set aside all your staff-based assumptions and orient your life, your thinking, and your recommendations to the perspectives, viewpoints, and issues of those you advise.

Failure to do this effectively will relegate you to being "just a PR guy," "just an HR person," "just a bean counter," "just a cop without a gun or a badge." Leaving your staff assumptions behind is among the hardest disciplines of being a trusted advisor. You will be working from a much broader perspective, first and always defined by the issues and questions facing those you counsel.

Although this reality was obvious to me from the early days in my career, it came home to me following a speech I gave in 1991 to the International Security Management Association in Florida. I was talking about my favorite subject, crisis management, to more than one hundred of the nation's most senior corporate security officers. The presentation and workshop lasted for nearly three hours. By the time it was finished and I had answered all the questions, I was late getting to the airport. As I checked in with my office within the forty-five minutes following the presentation, I had already received about half a dozen messages from participants. Although of course I like to think my presentations are powerful, important, and helpful, this was unusual. Once back at my office, I began returning the calls. It was clear I had said something really important during the presentation, but I was having difficulty figuring out what it was. So I began asking each participant who called, "What did I say that struck a nerve with everyone? My phone seems to be ringing off the hook."

The senior vice president of security for a Fortune 50 company replied, "That's easy. We were all buzzing about the comment you made that all problems in organizations are management problems before they are any other kind of problem. You were talking about the fact that if you want to successfully prepare management to deal with problems, you need to go to the CEO first, get his or her buy-in (through understanding what worries the CEO most), and proceed from there. You made the point that doing lots of preparation work and presenting a finished plan and process to management—largely developed by outsiders and even insiders— will probably be rejected by top managers and the boss, if not out of hand, certainly when problems occur—the worst possible time. I thought I could hear a hundred lightbulbs go on in the audience at the same time when you finished this portion of your presentation," he said. The calls were about helping these individuals, already very senior staffers, get the boss's ear for that all-important first conversation.

Each staff function tends to apply its staff disciplines to every problem it sees. Communicators look at everything as a communication problem; finance, as a finance problem; HR, as a people problem; security, as a problem of risk—you get the idea.

The principal reason staff people are excluded from operating meetings is that they bring too tight a staff focus. Most leaders, managers, and even supervisors believe they are good communicators, financially savvy, and aware of their surroundings. They assume they know the risks they face and can add, subtract, multiply, and divide. From the start, you are facing an environment that is not exactly staff friendly. This is a powerful insight. Dump the tendency to see everything through the lens of your staff experience. Yes, your perspective does matter, provided that, *first*, it reflects the attitudes and needs of the managers you are advising.

Let me put this into even sharper focus. One of the more frequent questions I hear from staff advisors goes something like this: "I need to know how to convince the boss to change something because big mistakes are being made. But the boss just will not listen to me. If a couple of the things I suggested are implemented, the boss would be much more successful in accomplishing his or her goals." My response to the staff person is, "Why are you pushing this so hard? Obviously, the boss does not want to take your suggestion. Unless what the boss is doing is immoral, illegal, completely stupid, or financially irresponsible, the boss is the boss for a reason. It is the boss's career and the boss's decision to make. Move on to something else. If what the boss is doing is immoral, illegal, irresponsible, or something along those lines, you have to address a professional employment decision." The message is this: remember who is driving the bus and whose bus it is. If you have a problem with this perspective, I suggest you put this book back on the shelf and look for something else to read.

See the Whole Board

If you have been tutored by or have taken classes from a skilled chess player, you know that one of the most important lessons is to keep the entire board in mind. You have to look at the whole board constantly as you plan and make your moves, assessing, analyzing, and forecasting the other moves that could result. As you have probably observed, some people are so skilled at this that they can actually analyze the board and predict how many moves are required to finish the game. Being a trusted advisor is very much like this concept of seeing the whole board.

Another way to think of seeing the whole board is to recognize the power of patterns. There is a discussion in much greater depth in Chapter Eight about pattern recognition as one of the seven disciplines. But at this point it is important to recognize that many things in relationships, business, politics, and human endeavors fit patterns of past events, in other venues or perhaps even in your own. Understanding the patterns of human behavior, the patterns of thinking, the patterns of events, the patterns of leadership, and the collateral issues these events trigger is another way to bring insight and understanding to leaders in ways far different from those they can achieve by themselves.

Your job as the trusted advisor is to look over the entire field of interest—the barriers, threats, constraints, options, and opportunities—and keep them in mind as you provide advice and recommendations to those you coach and counsel. You are consciously building the discipline of maintaining distance and altitude from everything that you talk about and recommend. Dispassion is a significant ingredient in establishing management trust, respect, and credibility in those with senior-level responsibilities. They need to feel that your advice comes with reliable objectivity, experience, and insight.

One metaphor to keep in mind here is always to operate at fifty thousand feet. Altitude changes attitudes. Altitude gives you an important perspective on every aspect of those areas that are in sight. It also builds dispassion and fosters objectivity. Some of the greatest insights you will have as a trusted strategic advisor are those driven by your ability to see a larger view, the more strategic view. As we will see in Chapter One, the leader's principal assignment is to look over the horizon and see what is there. When you too can observe from a significant altitude, you can see over the horizon to explore the environment that surrounds where the leader is looking and, perhaps, even beyond where the leader is looking. It is essential to maintain this sense of perspective.

Tolerate Constructive Ambiguity, but Strive for Certainty

Consultants and advisors are fundamentally option and alternative finders rather than solution finders. This is because leaders recognize that having a solution is oftentimes the least of their worries. What really matters is finding a process to get to something that works—almost anything that works. This is another area where the trusted advisor plays a crucial role.

Sometimes your role with a leader will be ambiguous, often because the leader's behavior is ambiguous. You do need to have a methodology for seeking clarification and for generating clarity. The more important point is that a leader's life is ambiguous and difficult. Solutions and answers seem easy for consultants, so it can be frustrating, irritating, and sometimes even embarrassing when leaders fail to grasp or intentionally ignore what is excellent, even achievable, advice. Develop a tolerance for what leaders instinctively know will keep them successful. The leader's ability to manage and to turn strategies into processes will lengthen the time required to achieve results, but ultimately will productively move the organization. Resist the common advisor frustration with getting the process part done.

Maximize Your Prerogatives

Being influential means having power. Getting things to happen today, when you want to or need to, is about creating immediate, visible impact through actions or decisions by the boss. You can also choose to be influential over longer time frames—whichever strategy best fits the objective you seek to achieve. A longer-term approach may mean less immediate impact. Some bosses are more comfortable with this style of counseling because they permit only limited visibility and credit sharing when workable ideas and decision options come from the suggestions of others. The ongoing clash of egos and ideas at the top often submerges the authorship of ideas. The benefit of this approach is that things that come out of top management are in the category of "being invented here." Though this can be frustrating for the advisor, this is the reality of working and advising at this altitude. The boss always gets the credit.

Actually seeing your recommendations become marching orders in real time is something amazing to behold and to achieve. Having impact tends to mean that the executive being advised or the group being counseled "does what you tell them."

The satisfaction of having immediate impact is often a central motivation for becoming a trusted strategic advisor. Leaders at every level constantly need special thinking, advice, commentary, and analysis in the achievement-focused environment that is today's "high performance" organization. There is the added reality that whatever you recommend must be doable using methods and approaches that operations can directly implement, and must produce constructive results promptly. The issue for the trusted strategic advisor is that his or her advice is always modified, adapted, and frequently used in fragments, with someone else taking or getting the credit.

It helps to be realistic about what leaders and their organizations can actually accomplish in a short period of time. Achieving operational impact can be difficult because the staff person is focused too far away from operations. The resulting lack of knowledge inhibits his or her ability to make powerful recommendations. This situation is buffered by the knowledge that many breakthrough ideas and solutions are extremely simple in nature and require only limited influence rather than an in-depth knowledge of operations or even finance.

If you are a more junior staffer, there is the nagging question, "If I'm several levels down from the big bosses, how can I get my ideas seen at the top of the organization?" The correct answer has always been to work through your current boss and your current boss's boss. Sooner or later, they will get tired of listening to you, and will instead send you to make your own case. Or they could fire you. In either case, a promotion, enhanced personal responsibility, or a constructive change in your career is likely. Successful advisors are self-selected, self-appointed, self-energizing, self-evaluating, and relentlessly persistent.

Teach your boss what and how to teach his or her boss. If there is no chance of this working, then there is virtually no chance of your getting information to the top. That means it may be time to look elsewhere for a position where your talents, knowledge, skills, and abilities can be better appreciated, or to grow in entirely different directions—whether within your own organization or, perhaps, somewhere else.

Develop Real Expertise Beyond Your Staff Function

If you want to gain access beyond routine staff consultations by operating executives, you must possess, perhaps above all else, some real, recognizable expertise. This expertise generally needs to move beyond your area of staff knowledge. The reasoning is that most senior operators feel fairly confident of their knowledge base in your area and assume that your competence in that area comes with the territory. If you stay within the box of your staff expertise, you will be called only when the boss thinks that staff expertise is required, usually to validate something he or she already wants to do in your area, and you will be told what to do and when to do it, what to say and when to say it.

Opportunities abound for providing special expertise, both from a staff perspective and operationally. In Chapter One, where I talk specifically about understanding bosses and boards of directors, you will learn about those special advisors who meet on a nearly daily basis about the organization they lead. You will learn about the kinds of information they seek continuously, and it may be that you can develop expertise and gather this information for the boss or other relevant senior officials. Once you have identified this special expertise and act to develop it, you will also need to develop a strategy to make certain that these special skills, areas of knowledge, or abilities are available to the senior leadership; we will talk about this topic in Chapter Ten.

Look around at those in the inner circle, those whom the bosses consult routinely, and ask yourself why these people are more sought after than you or your colleagues. One of the crucial reasons is that they bring this sense of real expertise to the boss's territory. If you cannot figure out why someone is in the inner circle, ask the boss why. The answer will be either very enlightening or totally underwhelming, but ask.

It Takes a Disciplined Approach

The lion's share of this book is about you and about how you will need to change yourself to be more successful as a trusted advisor. The chapters in Part Two discuss each of the seven disciplines you will need to develop, refine, or strengthen:

1. **Being trustworthy.** Earn the respect and confidence of those you advise.

2. **Becoming a verbal visionary.** Recognize that giving advice is an art and a skill that primarily depends on your verbal accomplishment.

3. **Developing a management perspective.** Look at the world through the manager's or leader's eyes.

4. **Thinking strategically.** This is perhaps the most valued quality of senior advisors—looking for methods and models to achieve different, novel, often unique solutions.

5. **Understanding the power of patterns.** Examine similar events to extract lessons for the future; the ability to understand patterns is sometimes referred to as the source of wisdom about what is going to happen.

6. **Advising constructively.** Provide advice using a structure, format, and context that can easily be both absorbed and acted on by those you advise.

7. **Showing the boss how to use your advice.** Showing the manager or boss how to put your advice into practice is essential. Most bosses learn how to work with advisors through trial and error. The best advisors always help their clients understand how to use the advice they receive from many different quarters.

Are You Ready?

One purpose of this introduction to the book is to help you assess whether or not you really have what it takes to achieve the role of trusted strategic advisor. In the assessment that follows, you will ask yourself some very serious questions to determine just how committed you are to becoming a trusted strategic advisor, or to see how far along you may already be.

Assessment: Are You Ready to Be a Trusted Advisor?

- Do I have the personal discipline to prepare myself to fulfill the five imperatives of the trusted advisor relationship?
- Do I have the stomach for the intense, conflict-ridden, and often confrontational environment in which decisions are made at the senior levels of organizations?
- Can I dispassionately assess the strengths, weaknesses, opportunities, options, and threats of the organization from a variety of useful perspectives?
- What is the real expertise, beyond my area of staff knowledge, that I bring to those who run my organization?
- Will I commit to mastering the seven disciplines and harness their power for my success and that of those I advise?
- How do I answer the question, "Why should the boss listen to me?"

Why Should the
Boss Listen to You?

Part One

THE REALITIES OF
ADVISING TOP EXECUTIVES

1

HOW LEADERS THINK AND OPERATE

The Pressures, What Matters, the Obstacles, and the Solutions

Chapter Outline

Pressures Leaders Are Under
    Leaders are having a lot
       less fun
    The limits of leadership
    The loneliness of leadership
What Leaders Do
    Focus on tomorrow

    Make it up as they go
    Handle daily intrusions
Why Leaders Fail
How Leaders Succeed
Study Leadership
An Important Suggestion for You
    to Consider

The place to begin our discussion on achieving the status of a trusted strategic advisor is to talk about the world of leaders and about how leaders operate. The environment of leadership; the expectations of leadership; the duties, responsibilities, and perception of leadership and especially of business leaders have changed in many important ways in the last quarter century. Becoming the CEO of a multinational company, a large local utility, a taxi company, or a dairy, or even to become the superintendent of the school district, used to represent the pinnacle of one's lifetime achievement. That, too, has changed. There are many powerful new realities that drive the world of today's CEO, as we will see in this chapter. Becoming a trusted strategic advisor in this changed and changing environment requires a clear sense of the new realities and of the role CEOs play.

Pressures Leaders Are Under

Let us look at the CEO's world. It is very, very different than most people imagine. All training for CEOs is on the job. There really is no school for becoming a CEO. A chief operating officer, watching from next door, second-guessing her boss, certainly thinks that she could run the place better. Yet the moment she gets the top position, the new incumbent instantly realizes that the job is completely different from anything that she could have possibly imagined. The new CEO also notices that she is alone, there is only one CEO in the organization, and everyone is watching.

Every single day for a CEO is a new learning experience because there is no manual and no one to train him. To his surprise, the CEO discovers just how limited his freedom to act really is. Wait a minute, you say—the CEO is the boss; he can do anything. The reality is very different. Being a twenty-first-century CEO is extraordinarily stressful.

Leaders Are Having a Lot Less Fun

A brief tour of today's executive leadership world will reinforce your understanding that these jobs are extremely difficult, challenging, and frustrating.

Studies by business organizations, executive search firms, and government indicate that the average tenure of corporate leaders is declining, as is the average tenure of their key staff. There are two patterns emerging, one global, one local. As larger organizations globalize, one of the most significant features is the youth of their leadership. For example, in nine global companies in which I have recently worked, each headquartered outside the United States, the oldest CEO is around fifty years of age. The downward trend in the age of CEOs puts pressure on the average age of managers and leaders in these organizations. In the past, a CEO usually got the job at around the age of fifty-five and held it until age sixty-four or sixty-five. Today, the CEO can be as young as forty-five or so, and may or may not stay beyond age fifty-five. It is a continuing trend that has yet to be clearly explained.

The second pattern is that younger people in general know a lot more than they used to, and at a significantly lower age. The amount of knowledge a thirty-five-year-old can bring to the business in the modern era is perhaps two to three times what it was just twenty-five years ago. These younger managers are indeed capable of leading large business organizations earlier in their careers.

In 2006, more U.S. chief executives changed jobs than in any other year in recent history. One-fourth left to take other CEO positions, one-fourth retired, one-fourth left on their own and went elsewhere, and one-fourth were kicked out. Special note: during 2006 and into 2007, a large number of CEOs resigned their positions due to scandals involving their complicity in option grant backdating.

Fewer than half of involuntarily retired executives regain a comparable position in their lifetime. More and more management literature is being devoted to these individuals and their inability to recover following sudden, unplanned separation from their top jobs.

Nonoperational issues—for example, global impacts, adverse legislation, and anti-corporate activism—are intruding with greater regularity. These interruptions are "soft" and highly emotional, and they require an entirely different attitude—frankly, one that goes beyond those taught by management schools. The Sarbanes-Oxley legislation, enacted by the U.S. Congress in 2002, introduced a distinctly moral focus into daily operations, an approach that continues to antagonize and irritate many business leaders. This legislated moral focus is frustrating for staff functions to discuss, decode, and decipher. Sarbanes-Oxley forced integrity and compliance concerns forward, basically through threat of criminal prosecution. This legislation has gotten management's attention at every level, but especially at the top, where the greatest risk now rests. These laws now mandate that managers of public companies are responsible for creating an "environment of integrity" within their organizations. These moral mandates are particularly difficult because they go against the grain of current management theory, which treats anything that is emotional, nonscientific, or not readily measurable as irrelevant and distracting.

Another nonoperational issue for large local and national companies, but especially for global companies, is the rise in power and influence of nongovernmental organizations (NGOs). NGOs are sometimes referred to as watchdog organizations. If they see something that offends them, they can go public, get activists to attack, or generate pressure from government. This has introduced a whole new level of stress, strain, and potentially negative visibility for business organizations and their leaders.

In large organizations, globalization increasingly requires staff functions to work together across intellectual, national, and cultural lines, and around the clock. It is definitely becoming more complicated to be a senior staff advisor in large organizations. The demands on the leader have increased significantly. On the one hand, leaders are asked to do more, faster; on the other, they are forced to reduce staff support, as an indicator of their management capability.

With all these distractions in the management and leadership environment, coaching and counseling leaders require important fundamental shifts in the advisor's mind-set. The trusted advisor needs to realize that the CEO, though still captain of the ship, is operating under increasingly complicated and uncharted navigation rules and pressures.

The Limits of Leadership

Deciding on a course of action is one thing, but getting the organization ready, willing, and able to move in that direction is an entirely different task. Successful leaders and their advisors learn to recognize the limits of CEO effectiveness.

One of the first large companies I worked for retained me to develop a marketing strategy for one of its highly technical product divisions, which was beginning to plateau as more competition entered the field. Another person and I spent significant time developing several unique approaches for the organization to consider. When we made our presentation to senior management, it was enthusiastically received. The senior managers were engaged in conversations; they asked questions and actually remarked at how sensible and important all the ideas we presented seemed to be. It was one of the best presentations I can recall making in all the years I have been a consultant.

We all went to lunch together, and I sat next to the CEO, whose name was also Jim. He seemed quite pleased. So I asked him, "With the reception this morning, how much of what we proposed is likely to be initiated?" Without hesitating, Jim said, "I'd guess about 4 or 5 percent."

I was absolutely stunned. "Jim," I asked, "did I make a mistake? Did I misunderstand what happened this morning?" Jim's answer was again quick and profound. He said, "Look, I'm just the CEO here. This place is run by the seventy-five hundred employees who show up to work every day. What they will want to do and can do will determine the direction we're going. I'm fifty-seven years old; if I stay healthy, I'll probably be chairman here for another seven to eight years. Absent some catastrophe, such as tremendous business loss, stock drop, or takeover, if I can move this organization five to seven degrees in new directions every year, I will have made a substantial contribution during my brief term as leader. We're kind of like an aircraft carrier," he said. "Once we choose a direction, it takes a lot of energy to change that direction. Of course, torpedoes, hurricanes, or collisions can make a big difference if they come along."

Leaders recognize and work to maintain the direction of their organization and what it takes to change, reshape, and perfect that direction. A leader's aspirations and behaviors often create a response among staff functions that causes people to overestimate the potential in situations and to be overly optimistic about results and about what can be changed. The leader's immediate staff often seem eager simply to move key organizational components or ideas around according to some checklist or set of theoretical ideas, based on what they assume the boss wants. The lesson of Jim's seven degrees is that the greatest successes are often the result of what first appear to be underwhelming decisions or actions. Although much is desired, far less can actually be achieved; yet meaningful progress will still be made. This relentless focus on meaningful but small incremental progress often yields big surprise advantages over the long term.

The Loneliness of Leadership

The concept of leadership loneliness will echo throughout the pages of this book. Several predictable consequences occur as an individual is elevated within an organization. First, the sense of isolation and loneliness tends to increase because fewer people are privy to information at higher levels.

Second, a filtration and sanitizing process occurs as information is passed up to the top. Mitigating this isolation of leadership is one key role for the trusted advisor. Jack Welch, being interviewed on public television shortly after he had retired from his chairmanship at General Electric, was asked by an interviewer, "What was the worst part about being chairman of this huge corporation?" Welch answered without a second's hesitation, "Being the last to know." This circumstance does tend to be a great frustration to those who lead.

Third, the higher the altitude, the thinner the leader's skin and the greater and more personal the criticisms they must endure. With increasing seniority can come decreasing tolerance for questions, questioners, those who push back, and people with negative approaches. This can be a fatal flaw in management leadership.

It is a major cause for isolation at the top and a powerful barric. the executive's knowing what really is happening at various levels in the organization. This behavior can be perceived as arrogant and intolerant.

Fourth, as managers advance and become senior managers and leaders, the "Yes, sir" mentality that pervades these high-level environments leads to the belief that leaders are good communicators, financially savvy, and aware of their surroundings and the risks they face. They have enough mathematical competence to get along. Absent sensible and meaningful evaluation, what else are they to believe?

In this environment, at this altitude, it is a principal role of the trusted strategic advisor to recognize these four circumstances and constantly, relentlessly, and endlessly help the CEO work against these patterns.

What Leaders Do

The CEO has three powerful assignments in any organization. The first job is to look to the future—that is, go over the horizon to see what is out there and then come back and tell the organization a bit about where it is headed; perhaps what some of the pitfalls might be; and, most important, what some of the deadlines are. The second principal task of the CEO is to find the people power required to achieve the organization's mission. Unlike the manager, whose job is to achieve objectives, complete programs, and work inside the box, the leader must work almost exclusively outside the box in this energizing arena of strategy, future accomplishment, and managing the destiny of the organization. The third assignment is to decide, to make choices. As the leader's career advances, his decisions become larger and the consequences broader. The leader's ongoing jobs are observation, education, course correction, evaluation, and motivation.

Leadership success depends on leader-driven communication. In fact, personal communication, in good times and bad, is the most powerful tool leaders have. When we examine how to move organizations, successful leader-communicators follow a fairly interesting pattern of mostly verbal communication and participation with their employees, executives, and others. The following is my empirical analysis of top management activity:

Analysis of Top Management Activity

Decision making	5%
Articulating the decision	30%
Coaching, teaching, motivating to carry out decisions	30%
Forecasting (guessing) the next decisions	5%
Admiration building	6%
Reputation repair	4%
Repeating, reemphasizing, reinterpreting decisions	20%
Total	100%

As you can tell by this distribution of time, the CEO and senior leadership will be spending significant amounts of time explaining, coaching, interpreting, reiterating, and monitoring the progress of their strategies, plans, and outcomes. This is far different from the notion that these senior people are busy making big decisions every single day about things that can change the company's direction or the company's history. Even during enormously stressful times, such as mergers, acquisitions, takeovers, or divestitures, the actual number of major decisions executives make is extremely small. It is the failure to communicate even these small foundational decisions that is often the root cause of much bigger operational failures.

Recently I was interviewed by a top management team for a very large company that was heading into labor negotiations. The prospects were fairly gloomy. The board was concerned about conflicting approaches that had been suggested, and they wanted to hear mine. When I finished explaining my concept to them, their first reaction was, "Well, Jim, from what you propose, we're going to spend a lot of time talking to employees." My response was, "What else have you got to do that matters?" They laughed as they realized that this was something of crucial importance and that they really had to make the time to get it done.

Focus on Tomorrow

Why is it that when the boss walks into the room, people's voices drop, everybody looks in his or her direction, and a sense of antici-pation tends to build? It is because the only one in the room who knows where we are going—in other words, who knows about tomorrow—is the leader or CEO who just walked in. We all want to know where we will be tomorrow. In fact, whenever a boss or leader enters the room, his or her first obligation is to share some of the latest news that only the boss gets to know or would happen to have. This is, in fact, one of the most powerful reasons why being a trusted strategic advisor is such an interesting position to hold: having that view, before anyone else, of where we are headed, which you can get only when standing next to and being around the person at the head of the line.

Leaders work in a future tense. The CEO is the chief strate-gist, and strategy is always about tomorrow's goals. This is because leadership is truly about tomorrow and what lies ahead. Contrast this with much of the staff activity in your own experience. Some people are busy defending yesterday and justifying things that have not yet happened, while still trying to leverage their way forward absent the kind of forward thinking and extraordinary insight leaders tend to expect.

Leaders avoid yesterday thinking because it can be very con-fusing and unproductive. Besides, yesterday is already owned by everybody else from their own perspectives. The past is owned by others intellectually, sometimes physically, perhaps financially, and certainly emotionally. And everyone's perception of yesterday is unique and often largely erroneous. The fascination of leadership and leaders is that most of their work is in territory yet to be owned or occupied by anyone. This is the definition of tomorrow, an intellectual area where people can come together and build their futures collaboratively. In current business language, we would say tomorrow is where it is possible to engineer new solutions and ideas. Tomorrow is where most people want to be in some positive, constructive way.

The trusted strategic advisor can only be a force for tomorrow. The closer you are in tune with tomorrow, the more compatible you are likely to be with the leaders you are advising.

Make It Up as They Go

One of the greatest surprises about leaders is that much of what they do is more or less made up on the spot. I discovered this early in my career, when I had the chance to coach the CEO of a large insurance company in the Midwest. To coach at this level, you have to meet the person you will be coaching ahead of the scheduled session, and there has to be an almost instant chemistry: Can you work together? Do you have the feeling that you are both on the same page?

My "beauty contest" interview with this CEO took place in his wonderful, exotic office on top of a very tall building. The view was amazing. The office had three full window walls; it was awesome. It was also really intimidating.

As we began talking, it was pretty evident that he had a "visitor management approach," no doubt because visitors asked the same questions about the view every time. The moment I started to speak, he took my arm, led me first to window number one, then around the perimeter answering all the questions about each wall—pointing out landmarks, history, useful detail—at about forty-five to sixty seconds per window. As he began explaining the third window view, my brain was screaming at me: "Say something really important, real soon. Only one wall left, and that one has the door you came through." My mental voice commanded, "If you want to get this job, you'd better ask an important question now."

So I managed to interrupt the CEO with a question: "Tell me something: Do you always know what to do? You run a company of fourteen thousand employees; I have a company of fourteen employees. My people expect me to solve today's problems and move ahead for tomorrow, following a plan. Do you know what to do every minute?"

He looked at me, smiled, and said, "Don't you ever tell anybody this, but I think the board actually hired me because I had a good sense of where we would have to go or need to go, and because at least half of my decisions would be carried out by people who really knew what they were doing. They felt that I could estimate, and make the right decisions in the gray areas at least 25 percent of the time. The remaining 25 percent they sort of left to me. They didn't have the answers for this either. For that particular part of my job, I am on my own."

"But I'll tell you something," he continued, pointing at the door, "every employee in this company thinks I have the answers. They think that I have a plan. I've got news for you: there really is no grand plan. We have only partial knowledge of how it is going to go. But if I were going to tell this to the people who work for me, they wouldn't believe it for a minute."

What I learned from that encounter, and it has stayed with me ever since, is that CEOs in particular are making it up about 25 percent of the time. They have to create what is next. They are making it up based on their experience or lack of it, on their concerns or their fears, and oftentimes on the perceived opportunities as well. This is an extremely interesting and powerful tool for advisors to have. When I am in meetings, and the meetings are wandering around off the track, once in a while I will turn to the CEO and ask, "Is this the part we know how to do or the part we are making up?" It is amazing how stunningly accurate this question can be.

Handle Daily Intrusions

There are tasks CEOs face every day that only they can handle, tasks that intrude on their day. These fall into four categories: soft intrusions, hard intrusions, nagging problems, and what I call career-defining moments.

Soft intrusions include negotiations with employees; anti-corporate government action; nagging negative news; personal, professional, or corporate embarrassment—real or potential; managing the moral decision-making elements of leadership; rumors; and unfounded or even founded allegations.

Hard intrusions are more operational in nature: a major stock price drop in a single day or in a single month; job actions and walkouts; major product market loss or product failures; other serious market problems; departure of a giant client or customer; failure to gain crucial government approvals; mergers or takeovers; and preparing for litigation.

Nagging problems are things like aggressive activist attacks, maybe on an individual executive or on board members; disgruntled employee or whistle-blower problems; negative trends in stock and business performance; persistent bad news; and bullying on the Web. These kinds of problems just sort of hang on and gnaw at the CEO every day.

Career-defining moments develop as a result of sudden stock price manipulation; criminal indictments; serious people failures; serious high-profile product failures, recalls, or deaths; and embarrassing, needless, obviously stupid events for which the CEO is held accountable.

It is amazing what takes up the CEO's day; nevertheless, these intrusions generally do fall into these four categories. It is helpful to use this category approach, because among your key functions is to identify, prevent, preempt, and correct these daily problems and issues and to suggest or develop solutions to them.

Why Leaders Fail

While we are talking about the CEO's main responsibilities, we also ought to talk about why CEOs lose their positions. At the present time, CEOs are losing their jobs faster than ever before. *Fortune* and other business magazines occasionally publish studies of the principal reasons CEOs are fired or asked to resign. Five reasons tend to stand out.

1. **Failure to deliver on what they promised when they got the job.** Boards of directors of businesses and organizations, as well as shareholders, are becoming increasingly inpatient with nonperformance. The risks are high, the stakes are high, mistakes are costly, and there is a lot of talent available these days to take on the visions of organizations. One of your key roles as a trusted advisor is to look for signs of nonperformance and bring them to the attention of those you are counseling.

2. **Excessive optimism.** CEOs and those around them tend to be overly optimistic in the way they describe their progress, minimize obstacles, underrate opposition forces, and deny the weaknesses in their organization, structure, strategies, and operations. Eventually, the metrics of performance or the truth from the line managers of a business will reduce and clarify whatever unfounded optimism CEOs and their advisors might provide. Here again, the role of the trusted strategic advisor is to take a sober, pragmatic view of performance and accomplishment to help the CEO deal in reality.

3. **People problems.** The CEO's key job is to find the right people and put them in the right jobs to accomplish the objectives. Failure to achieve this will cause the organizational effort to fragment or simply not to form. Teamwork suffers; people stop trying to pull together. Important talent becomes demotivated and unproductive—or leaves the organization. New talent becomes nearly impossible to recruit.

4. **Distractions.** CEOs sometimes take on too many roles on boards and commissions outside the company, spend too much time giving speeches, or become involved in other outside interests that get in the way of focusing on what needs to be done when they have big decisions to make.

5. **Stuck in the mud.** This is a somewhat mysterious category, but it has obvious symptoms: nothing is happening, there's no progress, and people may be leaving. For some reason, individuals who are extremely talented in one business environment sometimes fail by creating paralysis in another.

These five reasons for CEO firings show clearly what is expected of leaders. They need to deliver on the bold promises they made or on what the board expects, face and clearly define reality, build effective teams, stay focused, and be very good at figuring out what to do next.

How Leaders Succeed

What matters to leaders is success. They will pay attention to you if they think you have a good sense of what they need to achieve that success.

Every CEO and leader assembles her own set of ingredients—intellectual, financial, emotional, and behavioral—to drive her toward the success she seeks. In my observation of leaders and of the various behaviors that lead to success or to failure, I have concluded that there are five crucial ingredients, the absence of any one of which will severely impair a leader's success and perhaps even trigger additional negative behaviors by boards of directors and by constituents (employees, customers, or shareholders). Let's look at these five vital ingredients.

1. **Focus.** Focus is at the heart of what Price Pritchett calls the 95/5 rule. In our everyday lives, 95 percent of what we do probably does not really matter much. Focus means

relentlessly dealing with the 5 percent that is really crucial. I believe this is one of the most powerful disciplines of leadership—and when you consider the daily intrusions I outlined earlier, it is often one of the most difficult to achieve.

2. **Limit the number of objectives to be achieved.** We can accomplish only a limited number of incremental steps every day. If we are honest with ourselves, we recognize that it makes little sense to commit to a whole series of major objectives that we will be unable to manage because of each objective's myriad details. Working on fewer important objectives means taking a manageable number of incremental, achievable steps. Success is more likely.

3. **Build support and create followers.** One of the great downfalls of CEOs is the inability to manage the people dimension. They need to be surrounded with supportive people to make their work successful. People can stay together in support of the CEO if they can communicate constantly. Maintaining followers is a daily process because employees rarely know or care about what the CEO cares about or does. It is up to the CEO to verbally communicate what matters—with great intensity, continuity, and repetition. It is up to the trusted strategic advisor to help design the key decisions, strategies, and messaging to keep the pack moving in the right direction.

4. **Fix what is broken—fast.** Do it now. When things go in the ditch, pull them out now. If it is even likely that something might be cracked, broken, or slipping into the ditch, CEOs act preemptively to fix it now. A related concept is that of changing fast. In other words, if the marketplace is suddenly moving in a new direction, the CEO must move appropriately, move quickly, and, where possible, move ahead of the game once he or she understands where the market is going, or figure out a better direction. Fix it now, challenge it now, change it now, stop it now. Leaders learn that most strategies fail because of timidity, hesitation, and indecision.

5. **Finish what you start.** The number one reason that CEOs
   lose their jobs is that they do not or cannot deliver on what
   they promised when they got the job. So the critical skill here
   is to do less but to achieve more of that smaller number of
   goals. And for consultants or key advisors in particular, this is
   a very tough challenge because most of them are idea people.
   We are the folks who are always thinking up new things to do.
   For the boss, this is a problem. You walk in bright-eyed and
   bushy-tailed for your Monday briefing session, and you spend
   half that time laying out new ideas for the boss to think about.
   The moment you leave the room, he or she almost explodes.

   Not only has the CEO failed to finish the work he or she
   was expected to complete last week, but now there are four
   or five new ideas on the desk, which, it would appear, others
   fully expect the CEO to work with and potentially accomplish. Before a CEO can get to next week, this week and last
   week have to be finished first.

Ask yourself what you do when you are at the table with the
CEO or senior leaders. Do you push your staff function? Or do you
help them focus, keep objectives limited, build support, fix what
is broken, and finish the work at hand? If you are doing something
else, they probably think you are wasting their time.

I am occasionally asked, "Does the trusted advisor need to be
smarter than the leader?" The degree of intelligence is somewhat
beside the point. The fact is that the vast majority of trusted strategic advisors have little, if any, desire to be leaders. Their sole
goal is to be the best number two; the best associate and assistant;
the best helper, encourager, and success driver possible. For those
advisors who wish to be leaders, they should practice the ideas and
concepts recommended here, and those CEOs and leaders whom
they have helped will undoubtedly be instrumental in moving
these people along.

In my experience, it is far less likely that a consultant will
choose to become a leader over time, simply due to the fascinating
power, access, and insight that being close to a leader tends to

generate. There are far greater opportunities for trusted
than there are leadership positions available. By adjusting ....
expectations and temperament to achieve in these very influential
positions, trusted strategic advisors experience a very interesting,
dynamic, meaningful, and important professional life.

Study Leadership

If you are serious about advising people at senior levels, one of your
great preoccupations must become the study of leaders, leadership,
and leadership activity. It is surprising how few staff people truly
study their leaders or leadership, what operating people do every
day, and how leaders become and stay leaders. Studying leadership
involves a very practical and relentless curiosity about who leaders
are, where they come from, what their relationships are, and how
they came to be where they are. It also requires understanding
what leaders are trying to accomplish; what motivates them; and
how they think about various issues, topics, and circumstances.

An Important Suggestion for You to Consider

My suggestion is that you begin by looking at the kinds of
literature and sources leaders use to keep themselves informed.
The following is a list of publications that CEOs tell me they
routinely review:

Harvard Business Review
Forbes
Sloan Management Review
Fortune
Barron's
Wall Street Journal (every day)
Jack Welch's writings and books
Berkshire Hathaway's annual report (any year)
Directors and Boards

BoardRoom

Executive Book Summaries (monthly summaries of new business books)

When I've queried CEOs and other leaders about the most important business writers and thinkers, those they pay attention to, these are the names that crop up every time:

Peter Drucker

John Kotter (professor, Harvard)

Warren Bennis (consultant)

James Collins (consultant)

Tom Peters (business philosopher)

Joseph Rotman (professor, Rotman School of Management, University of Toronto)

Noel Tichy (author, lecturer, human resource executive)

Stephen Covey

Most leaders admire and read about or study other leaders—past and present. Identify those your boss cares about and then learn about them, too. Also read about and learn from other leaders who are of interest to you.

Take your pick. All these kinds of writings are extremely helpful in understanding the mentality, attitudes, behaviors, and aspirations of leaders.

Studying leadership should lead you to discover more interesting ways to be of service, to create more powerful and purposeful ideas and suggestions, and to develop a deeper understanding of how you can help those you advise achieve bigger and better things on a regular basis.

You may well find yourself in some fascinating discussion that explores what past leaders can teach the leader you are now advising. In the next chapter, we will look at what leaders will expect from you in this role.

2

WHAT LEADERS EXPECT

Chapter Outline

Now that you have a better sense of the CEO's world, it is time to think about what the boss will expect of you. As always, we begin by looking at those expectations from the boss's special perspective—that is, in terms of his or her goals, desires, attitudes, aptitudes, and attributes. For the trusted advisor, this perspective must become a permanent mind-set. Running through every chapter in this book and through the work of the trusted strategic advisor is the theme of having a management mind-set. This mind-set comprises several factors, one of which you have already been introduced to: studying leadership and leaders. Another is developing some real expertise in the business activities, strategies, and processes of the organizations whose leaders you are advising. The staff shortcoming most quickly noticed by operating people is the failure to gain any depth of knowledge or have serious interest in the actual work of the business. Nearly all the truly successful trusted advisors I have observed or worked with have cited their desire to learn key operational information, strategy, and background as among the most powerful relationship builders they have experienced.

> Learn something that matters about the business, and you will go a very long way toward gaining the respect and connection you will need to become a trusted strategic advisor.

The Boss's Special Perspective

It is the CEO who has the most open and complete view of the organization. Today's CEO sits on top of his or her organization's pyramid, on what is a very sharp point, as a matter of fact. In this uncomfortable position, he or she does have a clearer view than anyone else of every crucial aspect of the business's operations. Everyone else who is hanging on to the sides of the pyramid has at least a partially obstructed view. Moreover, every staff person who supports a senior executive has a view that is biased by his or her staff function or agenda of expectations.

David A. Nadler, in his September 2005 *Harvard Business Review* article "Confessions of a Trusted Counselor," illustrated the uniqueness of the top position by identifying five "no one else" factors that dominate the CEO's circumstances. No one else, says Nadler,

- Has a greater need for sources of unbiased information
- Needs to hear hard truths faster
- Is such a lightning rod for criticism
- Is the final arbiter in so many vital business decisions
- Is the subject of so many statements beginning with "No one else"

In contrast, "everyone else" lower on the pyramid is busy holding on to preserve his or her position in the organization or looking for ways to move higher up.

In the past, it was the duty of those just under the CEO on the pyramid to help stabilize this individual—during tough times, crosswinds, and gusty weather—for the benefit of the entire organization. Today, in many respects the point on which the CEO sits has gotten even sharper: those directly below the CEO are far less inclined to be stabilizers, particularly if something is happening that may diminish their chances of succeeding to the top of the pyramid. They are busy organizing for their own possible succession, protecting their turf, and, perhaps, keeping a peer from gaining any additional advantage.

This pyramid has sometimes been described with another analogy: the "monkey tree." If you are on the top of this tree looking down, what you see looking up at you is a bunch of smiling monkey faces. But if you are on the monkey tree somewhere down below, looking up, your view is quite different. Clearly, the best place to be on the tree is at the very top.

The Counselor's Prime Directive

Having been an advisor virtually my entire career, I have to confess my unending admiration for those at the top of the pyramid. Real leaders listen, hear, seek out many voices, and then extract from that huge menu of ideas and concepts the key insights or inspirations that will move an organization into the future. This is a crucial and amazing capacity of leadership. Few consultants and advisors have either this skill or the necessary temperament.

This acceptance and willingness to seek advice and inclusion is one genius of leadership. A part of that genius is the leader's ability to sift, to sort, to distill, to stratify and prioritize the ingredients of the future, and then combine the chosen ingredients so as to fuel progress.

The counselor's prime directive is always to look at the questions, issues, opportunities, and vulnerabilities from the boss's perspective first, and to test all advice against the leader's perspective. This approach leads to better, more usable advice, more quickly.

Useful advice has the following five vital qualities:

1. **Practical:** suggests tasks that are achievable and positive in nature and that employees and even critics can endorse to some degree.

2. **Pragmatic:** recognizes that only certain outcomes are possible, that no matter how spiffy, creative, or exciting your ideas might be, those affected by the advice as well as those acting on the advice will look at it from the perspective of whether it can actually work in their real world.

3. **Purposeful:** has self-evident forward focus and positive momentum. Counselors and consultants are strategic operational assets. When activated, strategic assets are fundamentally positive and energize the organization and its constituencies.

4. **Focused:** shows the way, helps the client or customer think and act in the future tense, and works toward a few important goals (or just one) that everyone recognizes.

5. **Fair:** is politically acceptable and politically useful (as opposed to manipulative or disruptive).

There are lots of distractions in consulting, and many clients have great difficulties, problems, shortcomings, and blind spots. The consultant's obligation is to identify and provide candid, constructive advice that fills those deficiencies, strengthens the shortcomings, and fills blind spots, while stabilizing or moving the organization toward tomorrow.

How the Boss Measures Advice

Those trusted few who spend a fair amount of time talking with, working with, and counseling leaders learn very quickly the strategic expectations of bosses. These advisors understand that leaders value only advice that has a positive impact on the organization. Before you offer an idea, concept, or recommendation to senior leaders, test your recommendations against these five questions:

1. Does it help the boss achieve his or her objectives and goals?

2. Does it help the organization achieve its goals?

3. If the answers to questions 1 and 2 are yes, is the project truly needed?

4. What aspect of the business will fail or fail to progress if the recommendation is ignored or delayed?

5. How does this suggestion save money, make money, or conserve money?

If you can keep your focus on these critical questions, your advice will be relevant. This approach puts you squarely in the CEO's shoes, looking at his or her tasks, challenges, and loneliness from a management perspective. Practice what I call the Counselor's Commitment (see the sidebar), and chances are that

The Counselor's Commitment

Those who successfully serve others have a work attitude that says,

1. When I am here, working for you is number one.

2. I plan to be here a lot and, if necessary, available the rest of the time as well.

3. I am committed to extensive independent reading, discussion, issue sensitivity, and personal learning that is of value to those I coach and counsel.

4. I will take the initiative to help those I coach and counsel move in useful new directions and rely far more on foresight than hindsight.

5. I recognize that going even a small extra distance will be the difference between mundane and magnificent results. Extra effort, extra sensitivity, extra focus are what make the difference from the client's perspective.

Read these five commitments carefully. If becoming a trusted advisor is truly important to you, then you must be willing to commit to each and every one of them. This is because the CEO has already made them to get to where he or she is. You have to make them, too, if you want to operate on the inside.

you will be sought after and respected and will have important influence on what the CEO does, what the organization does, and the success that the organization achieves.

What Bosses Expect from Strategic Advisors

What is really expected of you as a staff advisor? What are your obligations? The following are seven important contributions CEOs expect the trusted strategic advisor to make.

Real-Time Advice

If your methodology is to walk in, ask questions, take some notes, leave, think about things for a while, and come back, you are going to find that the CEO has moved on by the time you return. That is because at the CEO level, decisions are made and actions are taken pretty much in real time. You have to be able to give advice on the spot, or you will be invited back only when the boss has an assignment—that is, when the boss has figured out what he or she wants you to do.

Candor

I define candor as truth with an attitude. It is being super honest—promptly—and supporting that honesty with collateral information that matters. A candid advisor is willing to talk about anything, at any time, under any circumstances, and is willing to build transparency into every process, question, issue, or problem.

Coaching at Every Encounter

Coaching means taking the opportunity to guide, counsel, redirect, or direct the CEO in ways that are beneficial from his or her perspective, every time you are together. Suggest things that matter. Leaders expect substance, every time.

If you are in the room with the CEO or other leaders, you are expected to speak unless your role is designated as that of an observer. Your nonspeaking role will need to be explained by someone, preferably you. You are in the presence of leadership to provide something useful or be gone.

CEOs and leaders do notice whether or not you say something that matters, even when you are in situations with large numbers of voices present. They have a special sense about who is there and who is speaking. Even though some of these meetings can be intimidating—if not because of the CEO then because of the level, skill, and intensity of others in the room—if you are there, you are expected to offer useful advice on the spot. Failure to do so may mean losing your place at subsequent meetings until you can re-earn an invitation.

Consequence Analysis, Insight

You have to be able to interpret for CEOs the meaning of different aspects of a situation and the likely consequences and impacts of various choices. What is going on in the company's environment? Being a consequence analyst entails taking existing information that may seem commonplace or even irrelevant and extracting value in the context of running the business. You need to be a decision clarifier, a translator. You are helping the boss under-stand what is moving in his or her direction, what needs to be decided, and even the priority of the decisions that need to be made. Outside the boss's presence, you become an interpreter and explainer of his or her actions and decisions for other publics and constituencies.

Knowledge of What Is Important

As I noted in Chapter One, the filtration of information becomes so severe as it nears the top of an organization that most senior executives, but especially the CEO, are very concerned that what they receive is boiled down, oversimplified, sanitized, and detoxified. One of the trusted strategic advisor's crucial roles is making certain that key information makes it to the top very promptly, perhaps even ahead of everyone else in the organization.

Early Warning

In order to act more preemptively, the trusted strategic advisor intentionally has a different perspective on the interests of those whom he or she advises. It is likely that the advisor will be in early possession of information that could be helpful in avoiding danger or serious threats, or that signals opportunities and strategic advantages. This attribute of being intentionally different, of coaching and advising from unusual perspectives, may also provide earlier recognition that certain projects, programs, or ideas are failing and need to be stopped before they waste any more resources or send any more negative signals.

What to Do Next

A significant number of the decisions CEOs make are based on their ability to see where the organization is headed, to understand the real-time assets and liabilities of the organization, and to innovatively combine or supplement those assets and liabilities to solve problems or capture potential opportunities. CEOs always look for useful, sensible suggestions about what the next steps or increments might be. Such suggestions are among the highest-value contributions trusted strategic advisors can make.

Talents Advisors Need

Successfully meeting the expectations of CEOs and leaders requires six special qualities: initiative, inspiration, intuition, projection, loyalty, and urgency.

Initiative

The most common criticism I hear about both outside and inside advisors is that although ideas abound, few advisors seem capable of picking up an idea, developing it, and moving it forward without prompting or specific direction.

Initiative at very senior levels carries significant risks, and quite often the higher the altitude, the more risk averse individuals become. Because leaders must, for the most part, spend time waiting for things to happen, progress, or finish, those with initiative earn a higher degree of respect and attention than those without.

Inspiration

Inspirational people help others see (from the others' own perspectives) new truths and special insights that positively affect their emotions, behaviors, and beliefs. Quite often, unless someone makes a comment or reveals himself or herself, inspiration is a private moment of revelation between the individual who presents the inspirational opportunity and the individual who benefits. The isolation of leadership both triggers and inhibits the inspiration of new ideas and creative thinking. The trusted strategic advisor brings the inspirational ingredient to each encounter he or she has with the boss.

The ability to inspire is a quality that you can learn and develop. Identify those who inspire you. Focus on how they do it. Understand how they do it. Then use that knowledge to develop your own inspirational style. Inspire others. It is truly a gift that is appreciated, though often not acknowledged.

Intuition (Controlled)

Intuition is a charming attribute among the advisor's special abilities. It is difficult to develop and to cultivate. This exceptional quality of the trusted advisor—the ability to "see" solutions and next steps even in the absence of evidence and data—is highly prized. You can discipline yourself to develop your intuitive abilities.

Despite the importance of intuition, those who run organizations, especially large organizations, have a limited tolerance for intuitive solutions and recommendations. Managers today pride themselves on fact-based decision making. You must ration your intuition. Build support for what you intuitively believe or suspect. Present intuitive recommendations using a process approach so that you can be understood and your ideas can be acted on by those you counsel. (See the discussion of the Three-Minute Drill in Chapter Nine for a description of such an approach.)

Projection

Louis Pasteur, the great French scientist, was reputed to have said, "Chance favors the prepared mind." How prepared are you to hypothesize useful ideas, alternatives, and insights about the issues, concerns, problems, and work of those you coach and counsel? Do you read the publications they read? Do you consume information of the same type and nature that those you counsel do? Can you hold an informative conversation on an operating topic that informs the other person? Are you routinely ready to project yourself into the situations and circumstances of those you counsel?

Loyalty

The loyalty of the trusted strategic advisor comprises three factors: the alignment of fundamental principles of behavior, goals, and aspirations; the productive and constructive chemistry created between individuals who work well together toward mutually agreed-on goals; and a relationship based on candor and responsiveness to issues and questions that matter. Loyalty is an intentional, conscientious alignment of goals, interests, and actions.

Advising at senior levels also automatically makes you the eyes and ears for those you counsel. Your observations are a part of the information base that supports your advice. Successfully advising and coaching senior people requires a high level of personal candor both about the leaders themselves and about the what and why of what is happening around them. Loyalty is more than mere following; it entails actively engaging in the successful progress of leadership ideas and continually verbalizing and analyzing organizational behaviors, decisions, and actions.

There are limits to loyalty, which we will talk about in Chapter Four.

Urgency

Time is the universal perishable. Matters are urgent when time is a driving force or is used as one, when the loss of time has real consequences, when time may be running out. From an advisor's point of view, urgency means using time wisely by saying things briefly and powerfully. By using the pressure of time, the advisor constructively increases the importance of all actions.

Setting priorities establishes a sense of urgency. Resolving issues and problems quickly and effectively also creates urgency. Applying pressure to get things done at the earliest possible time, often for the most important of reasons, creates urgency.

Urgency is a double-edged tool. Used to motivate, inspire, and energize, urgency can be a constructive and productive force. Used to intimidate, badger, and bully, it can be destructive and corrosive, and can have long-term negative impact.

Do You Fit in the CEO Environment?

Now let's talk about whether or not you fit in the leadership environment. Here are some serious questions for you to ask yourself:

- Do I study leadership and the process of leadership?
- Do I care about these senior people?
- Do I have or can you develop a real interest and some expertise in the fields of interest of those you intend to advise?

- Do I care about what the CEO needs to have or to get done?
- Can I manage or set aside my problems and issues long enough to deal with senior leaders' problems, goals, and questions?
- Can I manage my own ego involvement in an environment where there are even bigger egos than mine?
- Can I make the Counselor's Commitment?

In the next chapter, we will take a look at the trusted advisor's critical tasks. You will not find them listed in any job description or anywhere in your organization. Sometimes the boss will clearly spell out what he or she wants, but most often it will be unspoken, which means you will need to figure it out.

Resources

Here are several resources I have found useful for learning about consulting and coaching CEOs and leaders:

- *Flawless Consulting: A Guide to Getting Your Expertise Used* (2nd ed.), by Peter Block (Pfeiffer, 1999)
- *The Flawless Consulting Fieldbook and Companion: A Guide to Understanding Your Expertise* (2nd ed.), by Peter Block (Pfeiffer, 2001)
- *Coaching for Leadership: How the World's Greatest Coaches Help Leaders Learn*, edited by Marshall Goldsmith, Laurence Lyons, and Alyssa Freas (Pfeiffer, 2000)
- *Control Your Destiny or Someone Else Will*, by Noel M. Tichy and Stratford Sherman (Currency Doubleday, 1993)
- *Power Vision: How to Unlock the Six Dimensions of Executive Potential*, by George W. Watts (Business One Irwin, 1993)

3

ACHIEVING MAXIMUM IMPACT

Chapter Outline

Gain and Keep the Confidence of
    Senior People

Speak Management's
    Language

Work Against the Patterns That
    Bother Bosses

Talk and Write to Time

Give Useful Feedback

Data

Perception analysis

Gossip

What to do next

People assessments

What Your Leader Expects

Do You Have the Discipline?

Viewing the world from the perspective of management rather than staff is the crucial prerequisite for establishing a sound relationship. There is always that nagging thought at the back of the boss's mind about consultants, counselors, and staff people: "Does this person really know what I do here every day, as they offer advice and counsel? Do they even care about what I want to accomplish?" I explained how to answer these questions in the previous two chapters. In this chapter, the focus shifts to your behavior and how you can achieve maximum impact as a trusted advisor.

Being listened to and having impact require that you gain the confidence of top leadership, understand and speak their language, avoid the typical staff shortcomings that annoy bosses, respect the boss's time, develop the discipline to structure your presentations, give useful feedback, and meet other expectations.

Gain and Keep the Confidence of Senior People

Typically, when I arrive at a client location, a variety of executives are tasked with briefing me on the situation. I learn about the individuals involved, the various relationships of the players, and whatever other information these high-level staffers think is important for me, an outsider, to know. Frequently, the focus of these discussions shifts from the problem at hand to criticism of the leaders; the staffers begin assigning blame for the current situation, speculating about the causes and sources of the existing environment, offering miscellaneous indictments of style, complaining of the failure to adapt or adopt preventive or preemptive measures, and generally assessing the leadership from the staff perspective.

Although undoubtedly unintentional, these are typical staff behaviors. And though I do listen to these discussions and, to some degree, take these matters into account, my inner voice is saying, "If I were your boss hearing this discussion, I would fire you on the spot." That is because this brand of thinking is fundamentally at odds with how the CEO thinks and what he or she expects. It is one thing to notice leaders' needs, deficiencies, and other problematic characteristics, but it is totally another to develop methods and techniques that address them constructively and promptly.

If you want to be listened to and have an impact, start where the boss believes he or she is. Focus, first and foremost, on establishing the relationship of trust and common direction with the boss. These are the relationship elements that matter. Mutual recognition of a common direction provides the platform for fixing various other shortcomings that may indeed be present. Truly understanding the boss's perspective may also illustrate to you that the concerns of staff people are far less relevant to achieving the boss's goals.

Some years ago I was retained by a large corporation to coach the chairman in preparation for a lengthy television series on his life as a senior executive. He was so busy that we scheduled three-hour sessions in a television studio to rehearse some of his stories and generally get him comfortable with what was going to happen.

The first session was to be held in the headquarters building in Stamford, Connecticut. He didn't show.

Nine days later, he had time on his schedule in San Francisco for a three-hour session. I traveled to San Francisco and got everything ready. He didn't show.

A week later, a third session was scheduled in Dallas, Texas. Same routine, same drill. He didn't show.

With just a few days to go before the actual taping was to begin, a session was scheduled in Stamford as a final attempt on the part of his staff to have him spend some time getting ready.

With twenty minutes left in the three-hour appointment, he came in the door, walked over to me, grabbed my hand, and said in his Texas drawl, "Hello, Jim, I bet you thought I was ducking these sessions on purpose." My response was, "Well, Rocky, the thought crossed my mind." He went on to tell me that the problem with what his staff had proposed for him, "media training," as he called it, was that when he spoke with his wife, Martha, her response was, "I've been married to you for forty-seven years and haven't been able to train you to do anything. How can someone you hardly know train you to be something different in just three hours?" Rocky went on to say that he had learned in his life to pay attention to Martha, but he wanted to make certain that I did not take it personally that he had missed all the sessions.

My response to Rocky was that what I had in mind was more along the lines of coaching, just to get him more comfortable and ready to deal with the two days of videotaping that would occur at the television studio. He replied, "Coaching, well, I can always use a little coaching." So we worked for the remaining time.

Following the airing of the program, his staff advisors sent me the videotapes to assess how he had done. From the first moment he was on camera, you understood vividly why Wall Street, the company's shareholders and employees, and others so implicitly trusted him. In his rather folksy Texas manner, he spoke the truth at every turn. He said things that were important, and he clearly had a sense of where the company was heading.

Rather than write the extensive critique his staff people requested, I told them that they should use the tapes of his performances for training other executives about how to be honest, honorable, extremely forthright, trustworthy, and visionary. Rocky was all of these.

It seemed that all his advisors were from the East Coast, mainly New York and Connecticut. For some reason they felt that a "good ole boy" from Texas, even though he was an extraordinarily successful businessperson, had to sound like he came from Connecticut in order to be an effective representative of the company. But Rocky knew what mattered, and he delivered.

Speak Management's Language

Some years ago, during a presentation by a communications firm that had recently been acquired by one of the large international consulting companies, there was a fascinating discussion about how the communications group was required to rethink their entire business model. They had two powerful objectives. The first was to describe their communications services, advice, and skills in much more management-oriented language. The second was to significantly reduce the number of potential service and counseling offerings so that all the consultants on the operating side of the firm and their client base could understand and utilize what was being offered.

The exercise the acquired communications group went through was quite enlightening, and its result was a focused list of services, expressed in management language and structured in ways that fit strategically into the other parts of the consulting operation. Here is how this new division described its management communication consulting practice areas:

- Strategic planning (formerly brainstorming and ideation)
- Customer-centered reengineering (formerly customer service)
- Executive and management development (formerly training)

- Staff development (formerly professional development)
- Team building (new concept)
- Organizational operational review and analysis (formerly communication audit)
- Corporate marketing and communications (unchanged)
- Crisis consulting (formerly crisis management)
- Exposure management and issue surveillance (formerly issues management)
- Employee loyalty building (formerly internal communications)

What difference does all this make? Each staff function—whether it is compliance, finance, human resources, law, security, marketing, public relations, or strategic planning—has worked to develop and use a unique vocabulary as well as specific concepts that are allied to management's goals. However, being allied to management's goals is different than being able to explain this valuable knowledge so that operators and executives can understand and use it more effectively when making important decisions. One of the great barriers, in my experience, to more effective staff utilization and input is the reluctance to describe staff functions in purely management terms. One reason for this reticence is that the inability to describe these staff functions in management terms may lead to questioning why a function exists at all, but that is another discussion.

This illustration demonstrates an approach that resonates with management and enforces a new level of discipline on the staff function to look at things from the management perspective. The point in this example is to limit the injection of extraneous ideas into management discussions and to make those that must be there important enough to be heard. Take the time to look at the services you offer and recast them effectively in recognizable management language. If you find them difficult to translate, what you are developing may be too staff oriented. Let it go or fix it.

Work Against the Patterns That Bother Bosses

In my discussions with chief executives and leaders, specifically about advice they get both internally and externally, a pattern of frustrations emerges relatively quickly. These are the most frequently mentioned frustration-inducing behaviors. You would be well advised to avoid them.

———

- Suggesting more ideas and concepts than can possibly be achieved or even considered. Remember that the most important reason CEOs lose their jobs relates to failure to perform. If your methodology is to suggest new ways of doing things or simply new things to do, you would be well advised to focus more on what needs to get done and what has yet to be completed rather than putting even one or two new ideas on the boss's desk.
- Engaging in time-wasting and nonspecific (purposeless) conversations. Even if it is the boss who brings up vacations, the family, or other chitchat topics, your role as the trusted advisor is to keep these encounters focused on what truly matters when getting things done. Yes, it is true that over time you will develop a relationship where a lot of personal information is known and seems appropriate to discuss, but my advice remains in force: keep these meetings and encounters as directed and professional as possible. Keep your actual role very clear at all times.
- Offering information that is late or incomplete, with some key facts and data or interpretations apparently being purposely withheld. Senior executives already know that the information they get is filtered, detoxified, and often pretty harmless. One of your most important currencies is candor, the important, concise, prompt disclosure of things you know that the boss should know. Information withheld or that is late for whatever reason reflects on the trust in your relationship. If there are even two or three incidents where your boss is left with the feeling that you are failing to be forthcoming, you will see your invitations decline.

- Offering information that is already known or that could be thought up independently. Stick to what matters. If you know that your boss already knows, move on. Count on it: you are wasting his or her time. Avoid doing that, or risk losing a good part of your relationship.

- Giving only partial input, apparently on the assumption that the boss knows more, or should know more, than he or she does. In Chapter Nine, I talk about a structure for giving advice with options. This was designed to prevent providing only partial information. To avoid leaving out key information, talk in terms of timelines or priorities: state what should be done first, second, or third, or apply a calendar or a clock to the information you have to share. This way, even things the boss already knows are put in a useful, more strategic context.

- Being less than candid. This behavior is a relationship killer. Whether a product of fear, lack of preparation, or simply timidity, lack of candor is the fastest way to become disemployed as an advisor. If you want to be there, be ready, be actively engaged, and tell the truth promptly.

- Failing to end meetings on time. It's better to have several smaller meetings that all end on time rather than one or two large meetings that put everyone behind schedule and accomplish less.

The problem with all these behaviors is that they distract and irritate top executives, and erect barriers to their taking your advice or taking you seriously.

Talk and Write to Time

Avoid the face-time fantasy. Too often, staff people estimate their value on the basis of the number of minutes or hours they spend in the presence of, or interacting with, senior executives. The only face time that truly matters is the time the staff person spends giving useful advice to an organizational leader. Yes, leaders often ask personal and personable questions. They appear to have a genuine interest in the individual who is advising them, and they really may. Nevertheless, for the most senior executives, face time is far less about getting personal than about gaining key information to stay in or get ahead of the game.

Always talk to time rather than filling time with talk. Find ways to limit what you talk about so that whatever your topic, you are ready to provide information in a format and fashion that is direct, helpful, and instructive. Talking to time means remembering that in English-speaking cultures, we say about 150 words per minute. Every document, every script, every written piece of information should be screened for its time requirement. This can be done very easily by putting a word count (using your computer's word count function) at the top of each page or document. Divide that word count by 150, and you have the approximate number of minutes it will take people to read the document or to present it. The operative rule is to say less but make it more important, and to write less but make it more powerful.

The more important the decision or the bigger the question or issue, the more likely it is that action will be pushed off until it has to be dealt with on an urgent or even panicky basis. The challenge, then, is to structure advice in a potent verbal or written format that saves time and helps managers make more strategic decisions. The Three-Minute Drill (discussed in Chapter Nine) is such a format. If you can commit to using it, it will change your relationship with your boss dramatically and help you have a much higher level of personal self-confidence.

Give Useful Feedback

To stay on course and to continue the evolution of their leadership, CEOs and managers need clear, useful, relevant feedback every day. Obtaining information that meets these criteria is difficult; few CEOs can do it on their own.

As I have pointed out, one of the more surprising realities of being the CEO or top executive is the change in information needs at this level. Rather than lots of detail and specific information, CEOs and senior managers need more evaluative and strategically relevant information. One thing we know is that at this altitude, the information CEOs and top managers get has been sanitized, organized, homogenized, and often made as inoffensive and generalized as possible. Information that could lead to decisions counter to the vested interests is often withheld completely. The feedback role of the trusted strategic advisor is one of the most crucial ingredients of an ongoing productive relationship with top management. You are the eyes and ears of organizational leadership. You are sometimes also the mouthpiece. While you are observing and collecting information and data, you will often find yourself, in return, interpreting, explaining, elaborating, or forecasting issues and actions related to top executive decision making. This goes with the territory.

Whenever I hear an advisor tell me that he feels like a snitch or that her assignment should not include observing and reporting back to the boss on what fellow employees are saying, doing, or feeling, I know this person will fail as a strategic advisor because he or she is failing the boss. Also, an advisor's being a snitch is never the point or the expectation of the CEO. CEOs do not have the luxury or time to engage in the politics that are common at senior levels. Instead, they need information to make decisions. Trusted strategic advisors have an affirmative obligation to pay attention to the surroundings of those they advise. This is solely for the purpose of ensuring that senior individuals possess the information and interpretation they need to better judge the future and the present and to characterize or extract whatever is useful from the past.

Let us briefly examine the five categories of information CEOs and top managers need daily from the trusted strategic advisor: data, perception analysis, gossip, some sense of what to do next, and people assessments.

Data

Data give the boss a sense of the market, a sense of the acceptability of the organization's goods and services. They can be financial, but the more useful data are yielded by the metrics of softer things like positive versus negative acceptance, probability, market velocity, or failure.

Perception Analysis

Analyzing perceptions involves gauging various aspects of the business—for example, the temperament of investors. What are they feeling? What are they saying? What are they telling other investors and analysts? What is the emotional state of the organization? What are employees saying? How are they behaving? Are we a happy ship? Is everyone having fun? Or is there a feeling of dread, doom, simply rearranging the deck chairs on the *Titanic*?

Gossip

CEOs absolutely love gossip. Part of its appeal is due to CEOs being out of the loop with so much of what goes on day to day in any organization, including their own leadership group. Another part is that to the practiced eye, the scuttlebutt is often an indicator of deeper issues or questions that the CEO needs to point out to the management team. The things management has only briefly thought and talked about out loud get into the pipeline easily and seem to go everywhere quickly. Grapevines are usually extraordinarily accurate and move with better average velocity than any formal communications program. The perceptions senior leaders have of what people are supposing, imagining, and hypothesizing are important in judging the organization's understanding of the key destinations the leader is asking everyone to reach.

What to Do Next

Typically, if you deliver the feedback that the CEO needs daily, almost immediately he or she will ask you a series of questions. The questions go something like this:

- What is your take on this information?
- What sorts of new problems, land mines, and potholes are out there relative to what we knew last week?
- What kinds of things should we be thinking about working through to resolve some of the issues this feedback indicates?
- Are there any immediate actions I need to take, or information I need to develop further, to help us stay ahead of what is coming into the organization or moving through the pipe?
- What are the three most crucial answers you need today?

People Assessments

Almost all CEOs and leading managers want evaluations of those around them, insiders as well as outsiders, and they will ask you as their advisor to provide them. Be ready with productive, constructive comments. Too often, I see internal advisors step back from this responsibility and, though often eager to criticize those who are outside the organization, speak only with great reluctance about those inside. Remember the number two responsibility of all people in leadership positions: have in place the people and skills necessary to achieve the goals and objectives the boss promised to accomplish. As a trusted strategic advisor, you want, always, to be in a position to make appropriate comments about everyone else on the team. Having a management perspective requires that you pay attention to what everyone contributes, the nature of what is contributed, and how those contributions can be improved. Be prepared to judge the capabilities and competencies of those in the leader's vicinity. All outside advisors can count on being asked to evaluate all inside experts and advisors. Be ready.

What Your Leader Expects

In April 2007, Larry Bossidy, former vice chairman of General Electric and CEO of Allied Signal, wrote a must-read article in the *Harvard Business Review* called "What Your Leader Expects of You, and What You Should Expect in Return." His article was aimed at other operating executives who work around CEOs. It contains a very instructive checklist that is highly relevant to the trusted strategic advisor. Bossidy suggests nine expectations of direct operational reports:

1. **Get involved.** Good executives know how to delegate.

2. **Generate ideas.** A person who is innovative and creative is a pearl to be treasured.

3. **Be willing to collaborate.** Surprisingly, many people still resist collaboration or sharing credit.

4. **Be willing to lead initiatives.** People are often reluctant to be associated with an untested idea, particularly if it crosses functional or unit boundaries.

5. **Develop leaders as you develop.** Too many people are selfish about their development.

6. **Stay current.** There is nothing more depressing than sitting in a business meeting with people who do not know what is going on in the world.

7. **Anticipate.** One consequence of failing to stay current is that you risk a setback.

8. **Drive your own growth.** I expect people to seek perpetual education and development.

9. **Be a player for all seasons.** It is one thing to sustain these behaviors in good times. How do you behave when they are in decline?

Bossidy's approach serves as a thoughtful and insightful guide for those who advise leaders, just as it does for those who are leaders. Each of these suggestions helps engage the leader and the advisor with each other. For the strategic advisor, these activities broaden and deepen his or her ability to develop more operationally effective advice.

Do You Have the Discipline?

As should be apparent by now, maximizing your impact means truly focusing on what really matters to management. This approach is what will help you gain and keep the confidence of senior leaders. Resist joining in with the typical staff complaints about senior management's weaknesses and blind spots, avoid falling back into staff talk, use the boss's time effectively, and carefully structure your verbal recommendation presentations. As you contemplate what is expected of you, ask yourself some hard personal questions and answer them candidly. They will help you develop a productive level of personal discipline and intensity, and they enable you to anticipate, even trigger, the kinds of questions that build your relationship with those you advise:

- Where necessary, how will I fill management's blind spots and suggest ways to overcome management's limitations?
- How do I separate myself from my own predispositions, assumptions, and antimanagement biases?
- What habits do I have that add positive energy to what management has to accomplish?
- How skilled am I at moving different constituencies to listen and act?
- What is my personal strategy for building management's expectation of strategic contributions from me?
- Can I manage my own ego involvement in the circumstances I encounter?

These are tough questions for most of us because we naturally focus on our own needs ahead of management's. When we develop the discipline to focus on management's needs first and foremost, we maximize our potential impact on management. Leaders notice.

Part Two

THE SEVEN DISCIPLINES

4

BE TRUSTWORTHY

Chapter Outline

Trust has various synonyms, such as reliability, confidence, and credibility, all essentially saying that one can count on the performance or behavior or thinking of an individual. My take on the word, though, is that trust is simply the absence of fear. Fear is negative, detrimental, corrosive, and sometimes toxic to relationships. Fear may cause the boss or leader to ignore, preempt, suspect, or resent the ideas of others, even ideas from advisors who have historically had access and credibility. When trust is lost, suspended, or damaged, the offender is put out of the inner circle.

Trust Matters

As you move up in authority, responsibility, and power, trust becomes increasingly crucial because this ingredient in the relationship is what permits, sanctions, and protects interpersonal openness, candor, truthfulness, and face-to-face engagement. The stakes are always high in the relationship dynamics between trusted advisors and the leaders who rely on them. Serious ideas, issues, or money, and even the future, are always on the table. At the senior executive level, there is also a sense of "Either you're with me or you're someplace else." Neutral ground is hard to find at the altitude of senior executives. An environment of trust helps to constructively channel emotions and thinking.

Trust is one of the important reasons people are promoted. Sometimes trust has more weight than actual competence or accomplishment. Many senior executives I've worked with have selected surprising people as true confidants. These trusted individuals may or may not have relevant business experience, but somehow the boss has come to rely on their judgment, observation, or insight. It also helps if the trusted individuals pose no particular threat, even when they challenge the most cherished beliefs or inclinations of leaders.

Loss of trust is one of the unstated but primary reasons people are demoted, fired, or just ignored. Why? Generally, the higher the altitude in management, the lower the tolerance for mistakes in judgment. Apparent attempts to usurp power to which one is not entitled, and the exercise of authority without support from another leader or established internal benefactor both get a negative reception. One is tempted to call this politics. Politics certainly is a useful analogy at senior levels, because for an advisor to be trusted, especially during times of stress and change, he or she must be able to manage the politics of relationships, including those among senior leaders.

It is worth noting that most managers and leaders rely on their advisors to develop the necessary relationships among the other managers and executives surrounding them, so that the advisor's ideas can be accepted by all rather than appearing to be designed merely to please the manager or boss. While reviewing this manuscript, one chief executive mentioned that she has repeatedly had to caution an advisor that pleasing her, though important, was only one ingredient in successfully advising at the upper levels of management. The advisor was expected to build relationships with chief financial officers, legal counsel, strategic leaders, and the handful of other top people who advise the senior executive. It is the rare consultant who can work exclusively for the CEO and survive for any length of time while ignoring the concerns, issues, questions, and relationships of those near the top.

An advisor is trustworthy because he or she is helping and advising for the obvious benefit of the other person. From the trusted advisor's perspective, his or her work is always about the other person. One general axiom of relationship success might be stated, "When you help others get what they want, they will help you get what you want." This is absolutely true in the business of strategic consulting and advice giving. Waste time, misjudge your relationship, fail to help, seem self-serving, or exploit your proximity to power, and the relationship of trust will suffer, or you will earn the negative attention of other senior players in the process.

A question I often hear, especially from more junior aspiring advisors, is, "How old do you need to be to be heard and trusted, or just to get in the room?" There are, in fact, many examples in the business world, in academia, in key professions, and in government indicating that competence, expertise, and the ability to convey critical information effectively matter more than age. Some examples are Steve Jobs (he started Apple at age twenty-one), Bill Gates (Microsoft became an independent company when Gates was twenty-one), and Warren Buffet (he taught Investment Principles, a night class at the University of Nebraska, at twenty-one). More contemporary examples include the young founders of Google and Yahoo.

Having spent some time in government service and much more time in the private sector, I can tell you that being trusted and being effective are rarely about age. Being trusted, at least at first, is about service to others based on some specific, unique knowledge or aptitude. It's about demonstrating competence even if the area of knowledge is narrow. In fact, the truly general business expert is a rare commodity. Most expert advisors have a limited spectrum of knowledge and experience. What makes them successful is their ability to use their expertise as a platform to have maximum management impact.

The answer to the age question is, "It's about what you know and what comes out of your mouth rather than the grayness or absence of your hair" or, for that matter, your years of experience. The continuous and relentless expansion of knowledge, especially in developed cultures and societies, means that younger people know a lot more than someone more senior knew at the same age. Each generation is better informed and pushing upward faster with a more strategic value in its knowledge base. Thus the greatest challenge for the rising star is building the trust component of his or her relationships rather than gaining adequate knowledge. The individual who can provide intrinsic wisdom will gain the necessary knowledge and experience over time. Up-and-comers appear too often to be more interested in their own career trajectory than in the crucial tasks managers must accomplish. Remember, the needs of those you advise must always come first.

Trust and Influence

Having influence means that when the advisor speaks, recommends, challenges, or teaches, decisions will be affected in almost every case. Sometimes just a look between the trusted advisor and the powerful person is enough to change the flow of events or decisions. Real influence is built incrementally over time, mostly through the advisor's initiative. One potentially dangerous benefit of having influence is that those around you, those below you, and even those above you recognize that you have this special ingredient in your relationships with those you are advising. The potential drawback of having influence over important individuals and events is the very interesting and serious level of risk you can incur. Those around you who may not be trusted or who have their own agendas or access problems will come to see you as a potential conduit for influence of those you advise.

Influence always attracts the attention and focus of those further away from the centers of power. Another interesting aspect of working at very high altitudes with access to unique and unlimited information is that you become mindful of the proliferation of agendas being pursued around those who make the most important decisions. Influence and access attract the attention of those who don't have either. A trusted strategic advisor has to be able to manage the internal politics of access that inherently exists at senior levels. And there is always politics up there.

Trust and Loyalty

Trust, influence, and loyalty are linked. Having a boss trust you is the basis for access (access to information and meetings); access facilitates influence over the boss; influence over others often is also possible if you are loyal to them. Trust and influence in the advisor's relationships create the perception of loyalty in the minds of those being advised. Loyalty matters at all levels of management because the number of followers matters. The ability to effect change and progress depends on the loyalty of individuals near the top and at many other levels of the organization.

There was a scene on the NBC television series *West Wing*, which is principally about White House staff people, in which one of the president's senior staff people was about to suffer a huge public embarrassment, possibly leading to his resignation or termination. In this fictional environment, like many real-life environments in large organizations, when those who are important have big problems or are even rumored to have big problems, it is customary for colleagues nearby to step away and leave the afflicted individuals to fend for themselves. The person either rises or falls based on his or her own actions, responses, or past deeds.

In this scene, Leo McGarry, the president's chief of staff, meets with the key individual and tells him a powerful story that went something like this. "A man is walking along and falls in a great big hole. After he picks himself up and figures out what happened, he realizes he's trapped, and he starts to shout for help. A few minutes later, a workman walks by and, hearing the man's shouts, looks into the hole and makes a couple suggestions about how he might dig his way out or climb his way out. A little while later, a young woman comes by, looks in the hole, and says she will find some help and call 911. More time goes by, and a priest, hearing the man's shouts, looks into the hole and writes a prayer on a piece of paper, then drops it in the hole to console the man. Then a longtime friend walks by, hears his friend's shouts, looks in the hole, and jumps in. The man in the hole looks at his friend and says, 'Now see what you've done; we're both stuck here.' His friend looks him in the eye and responds, 'Actually, I've been here before, and I know the way out.'"

McGarry's final remark puts the punch line on the story. He says to his friend, "As long as I have a job, you have a job." This is an example of how trust fosters loyalty, and loyalty turns out to be the glue that holds the trusted relationships together, especially when there's trouble.

Establishing trust in the first place is the tough part. It is by far easier to recognize those behaviors, behavior patterns, and attitudes that damage trust and personal credibility. Put in a more interesting way, trust, like loyalty, is fragile and magical. Both are products of good relationships.

Loyalty Has Limits

The executive staff ranks are full of strong-willed people who choose or learn to be loyal to the CEO. That loyalty may be situational (for example, choice) or pathological (for example, brownnosing), depending on the person.

In the case of the trusted strategic advisor, the relationship with the senior leader is less about blind loyalty and more about a higher level of objectivity and perspective. By keeping perspective I mean always remaining at some altitude, some constructive distance to ensure that the advice given or taken is truly the most valuable and most helpful. Being objective can, at times, seem less than loyal. This perception occurs most often when the senior executive is choosing between admitting something and hiding, deferring, or otherwise delaying that something—in other words, when there is dilemma between disclosure and denial or between confirming negative events, decisions, or outcomes and trying to paint them in a better light. In most of these circumstances, the most junior employee in the organization can suggest or recommend the correct course of action, but it takes the relationship weight of the trusted advisor, bearing down on this very senior person or group, to generate the impact necessary to get the correct decision made. In giving the best advice or counsel, the trusted individual is willing to take risks based on that trust, including termination of the relationship should that be required.

In one of the few times I have involuntarily lost a trusted relationship (and was fired), I had been working for a couple of years with a fast-growing technology company in the Southwest. Abruptly, the CEO decided to retire, and a new one was brought in, someone who was new to me and to whom I was new.

Over three or four weeks we worked together on a couple of projects, and I generally thought we were beginning to put a relationship together. Then he called me on a Friday afternoon and asked me to prepare announcements for Monday about laying off approximately six hundred to nine hundred people. As it happened, the company was already growing so rapidly that there were at least five hundred to six hundred current openings for positions all across the organization.

Over the weekend, I drafted a tightly drawn, well-thought-out one-and-a-half-page e-mail describing how we could easily shift many of those slated for departure into the open positions already available and in need of occupants. At the time, I thought I was providing the type of service the CEO was looking for in a trusted advisor.

However, on Monday, I received a very short response; it was, in fact, just five words: "You're not on my team." Translation: "You're fired."

What I failed to grasp in this new relationship was that this individual, unlike his predecessor, was brought in to sell the company, not to grow it. I simply should have known better, should have found out or paid better attention. I should have asked good questions before I launched forth with my recommendations. Maybe it was Stephen Covey who said, "Seek to learn before you speak." It was my fault, and the CEO probably felt that he didn't have time to bring me up to speed or that I should have figured out his agenda on my own.

In another case, the chairman of a Fortune company I was advising had just been indicted, after two and a half years of bad news, embarrassing experiences, and fear. He expressed his relief to me and said that finally, having been indicted, he could now settle down and do the things in his community he had been unable to do previously because of his busy life and, most recently, the criminal court case. I could hardly imagine what was on his mind aside from preparing for his defense, so I asked him. He said, "Jim, for years my name has been on the rosters of many local civic organizations, when all I did was to have the company write a check. Now I can actually get involved and put some of myself into these groups." My response was immediate and candid: "George, tomorrow morning your wife is coming over to your new office [now outside the corporate headquarters], and you will call all of these organizations and resign immediately. None of them can afford to have an indicted potential felon connected to them in any way. If you don't call them, they'll call you and do it." He made the calls.

Set Personal Loyalty Limits

Another reason that loyalty has limits is that not all CEOs are honest. Some have committed or are committing crimes. As we approach the end of the twenty-first century's first decade, there seems to be a mass lapse of integrity among corporate leaders in America. The U.S. Justice Department and attorneys general in the United States are prosecuting more corporate executives than ever before. Most of these individuals have advisors.

A powerful example of this integrity lapse is the continuing scandal regarding the backdating of stock options. As these situations unfold, the CFO has to go because he suggested it and figured out how to do it. Then the CEO goes because he agreed to it and permitted it to occur. Finally, the general counsel is fired because she pronounced it a legal action for the organization to take. The companies involved pay big penalties, and, of course, it is the shareholders who bear the brunt of the cost and damages.

The key question for you as the trusted strategic advisor is, what are the indicators that should cause you to question your loyalty or, at a minimum, raise serious questions of those to whom you provide advice? There are patterns of suspect organizational behavior to look for that, ironically, generally begin in the top executive ranks. The presence of even one or two of these indicators in your working environment is a very serious matter.

Ask any prosecutor: if allowed to continue, persistent unethical behavior, even on a small, very limited basis, will very likely lead to criminal behavior. The Federal Sentencing Guidelines of 1991 list fifteen of what are called predicate behaviors, inappropriate activities to look for that signal serious potential trouble. Here's a sampling:

Lack of tough, appropriate, centralized compliance within areas of the company

Leadership that allows supervisors to overlook bad behavior

Structuring incentives in such a way that they can compromise the ethical behavior of people or the quality of products and services

Permitting shortcuts to be taken for a variety of obviously questionable reasons

Ignoring rogue behavior

Toleration of the inappropriate behavior of management by individuals who are "critical to the organization's mission"

An emphasis on "doing whatever it takes" to achieve appropriate business and financial goals

Belittling or humiliating those who suggest or seek ethical standards

One other comment about the limits of loyalty: whenever you are sitting in a meeting or discussion and you know you couldn't tell your mom or your kids about it, or you feel you need an attorney, first try to shut down the conversation, but then you should probably leave and go find a lawyer quickly.

Establish a personal integrity barrier, your own loyalty limits. Write them down and be prepared on a moment's notice to explain those limits. This exercise alone will prepare you to provide a service of extraordinary value to those you advise if it prevents, helps detect, or deters activities or plans they will later regret or that could cause harm to others.

Where do you suppose all those former trusted strategic advisors to convicted or dismissed executives are? They are probably wishing they had spoken up much, much earlier.

Trust-Appreciation Confusion

Many advisors suffer from a sense of confusion: their advice may be taken, even relied on, yet they feel that their work is not appreciated and that their contributions and their presence are undervalued. The questions I hear are, "Why aren't there more expressions of appreciation and acknowledgment?" "How can I get [the boss] to acknowledge my value?"

My first response may seem a little flippant, but it usually goes something like this: "If you're in the business of being a trusted advisor for the accolades, recognition, and appreciation it will generate for you, you'd better choose another career direction as quickly as possible, because you'll be waiting a long time." This issue is similar to what I described earlier as the face-time fantasy.

Proximity to power is a false indicator of real value. It's the actions leaders and managers take based on your advice that counts. You'll have to do the counting if it really matters to you.

The Ingredients of Trust

Trust involves at least five crucial ingredients. As I define them, you'll note that many of these ingredients are also a part of leadership, followership, and relationships in general:

1. **Candor.** Truth with an attitude, truth plus insightful and honest perspective; for example, there may be other perspectives on the same set of circumstances even though the facts seem to apply across the board. Candor also takes other perspectives into account.

2. **Credibility.** Always conferred by others on those whose past behavior, track record, and accomplishments warrant it. You deliver what you promise.

3. **Competence.** The ability to apply special knowledge, experience, and insight to resolve the issues, questions, and problems of others; putting the power of your intellect and expertise to work, clearly for the goals of another.

4. **Integrity.** The personal, organizational, or institutional inclination to do the right or most appropriate thing at the first opportunity or whenever there is a choice or dilemma. A person with integrity is someone you can count on to steer you in the right direction or help you make the morally correct decision, often on the spot, every time.

5. **Loyalty.** Faithfulness, sometimes devoted attachment; often involves a genuine affection for the individual or circumstance, and a willingness to go anywhere, do most anything, follow the lead given, and spontaneously speak up for someone and his or her beliefs.

Establishing Trust

It is extraordinary how the process of establishing trust is similar in situations and relationships between individuals, between individuals and organizations, between organizations themselves, between organizations and society, and even between cultures. It has been my experience that establishing and maintaining trust is a process, one carried out with directness and simplicity. Trust is the result of taking sensible, simple, constructive, and practical steps. There are six elements in establishing and maintaining trust:

1. **Provide advance information—a "heads up"—whenever you can.** Providing advance information is the first and most important ingredient because its absence has one of the most toxic impacts on relationships. You trust another individual above all else because of his or her willingness to anticipate those situations that could be negative or threatening. In the context of senior leaders, providing advance information means making certain they have, from you, the information they need to achieve their objectives or to defend or deflect actions or perceptions that could be detrimental to their success or progress. They expect to be warned of danger, damaging decisions or threats, potential disasters, and disloyalty.

2. **Seek the leader's input.** Asking for input is the second most powerful ingredient of trust. Those being asked are also receiving a signal of their value to you. Taking action without asking for or seeking input is considered to be arrogant and unempathic.

3. **Listen carefully.** Careful listening is driven by the conversation or the information that is exchanged, by the constructive and open nature of the questions that the listener asks for clarification, and by a real sense that each individual or organization is engaged in the conversations that take place during the relationship. Trust depends on careful listening, from every side.

4. **Change your approach based on what you hear.** When you change or modify your plans or expectations as a result of listening and input, you further demonstrate that you can be trusted. Changing previously announced actions, planned behaviors, and outcomes evidences active engagement, paying attention, and reflecting what is heard.

5. **Stay engaged.** Maintaining trust is an ongoing, interactive process. Rather than waiting for others to contact you or maintain the relationship, you call, on your own behalf and in the other's best interests, to keep the relationship moving, alive, and essential.

6. **Engage others.** The most powerful gesture you can make to build trust is to invite those affected by your decisions and authority into the decision-making process. At the very least, inviting them to "look over your shoulder" while important decisions are made is enormously reassuring and fear reducing.

The wise advisor helps leaders recognize that their own ability to establish, maintain, and restore trust rests on these same six actions.

Busting Trust

People often assume that once a bond of trust is established, it is difficult to break. Experience demonstrates that a bond of trust, once established, generally makes reestablishing a relationship easier, but the bond itself is fragile.

Trust does seem a bit mysterious. It is far easier to identify the behaviors and attitudes that damage it. Earlier in this chapter, I defined trust as the absence of fear. As you'll note in the list that follows, fear is quite logically the absence of trust. Fear is what fills the vacuum when trust is questioned, damaged, or destroyed. Here is a top-ten list (in alphabetical order) of the most frequent and most easily avoided trust busters:

1. **Arrogance.** This is displayed through the practice of presuming permission for making decisions unilaterally without input from key partners.

2. **Broken promises.** Trust means that each party can rely on the commitments of the other, both implied and explicit. When those commitments are broken without prior notification, understanding, explanation, or warning, the first element of the relationship to suffer is trust. Losing the safety of commitment will call into question most other elements of the relationship.

3. **Chest beating.** Unwarranted self-congratulatory, self-validating behavior puts distance between those who want to trust and those who need to be trusted. It's a form of self-deception.

4. **Creating fear.** This usually occurs when one party damages or threatens to damage the other, without the other's permission or advance knowledge. Fear includes feelings of dread, helplessness, even betrayal in the relationship.

5. **Deception.** Misleading intentionally through acts of omission, commission, negligence, or incompetence creates feelings of separation, distance, and disappointment.

6. **Denial.** This means failing or refusing to promptly come forward and acknowledge the circumstances, mistakes, and errors in judgment that produce negative surprises.

7. **Disparagement.** Often a subtle form of blame shifting, disparagement is easily recognized by negative words and descriptions, such as "He's uninformed," "They just don't understand," and "They wouldn't listen."

8. **Disrespect.** Even adversaries can trust each other to some extent, provided there is a sense of respect. When the reputation of an individual, product, or organization is minimized, trivialized, or degenerated, there is a sense of uneasiness and discomfort that often leads to frustration, anger, and more negative behavior.

9. **Holding back.** The essence of trust is having information or confidence in advance of decisions and circumstances so that no matter what happens, those in the relationship can count on each other's behaviors and attitudes. Deliberately withholding information, support, admiration, cooperation, or collaboration destroys relationships.

10. **Minimizing danger or the significance of events.** Using or parroting such phrases as "It's just an isolated incident," "We are not the only ones," or "If we don't do it somebody else will" and failing to accurately and realistically identify faulty thinking, stupidity, and serious problems can lead to mistakes and further errors for which the advisor loses the trust of those relying on him or her, and the bad behaviors continue.

For the trusted strategic advisor, this is a list of warning signs, indicators, and potential threats to existing trusted relationships. Watch out for them; avoid, prevent, or preempt them. Maintaining trust requires constant analysis of the relationship to identify and eliminate negative behaviors, confusion, negative attitudes, and unexpected outcomes. It entails a personal commitment to loyalty and a driven sense of long-term interest in the relationship and in achieving the boss's goals and aspirations.

Questions to Consider

Ask yourself these questions to help you rethink, review, and reconnect with the key topics in this chapter:

- Do I put the interests of those I advise first?
- Are my values clear, both to myself and to those I advise? Do you live by them?
- Do I have the competence I advertise?
- Am I always on the boss's team?

- Do I recognize, understand, and care about the boss's goals and aspirations?

- How prepared am I to take the actions necessary to repair the damage once trust is broken?

- How often does my boss take action on my advice?

- How many of the ten trust busters have I witnessed, committed, or condoned (and how often)? Can I think of other behaviors and attitudes to add to this list?

- What are some ways I can implement the six elements of establishing and maintaining trust in my professional relationships?

- Am I prepared to stand up when improper, unethical, or potentially dangerous decisions are being considered or implemented?

- Have I thought through carefully the limits I place on my loyalty to those I advise? Have I put these limits in writing so that I can explain them and share them with others?

5

BECOME A VERBAL VISIONARY

Chapter Outline

Jack Welch, the former CEO of General Electric, is an excellent model of the modern, highly verbal executive. His life and work, as described by him and others, provide a rich mixture of both complex and extremely simple but powerful lessons for those of us who are trying to run our organizations and advise others. In his first book, *Straight from the Gut,* Welch talks about one of his early essential goals as he took over GE: the elimination of a vast midlevel bureaucracy that enveloped anyone with career potential and chained his or her life to notebooks under the command and control of various midlevel managers, human resource staffers, and others. Throughout an employee's career at GE, his or her experiences, infractions, successes, muddles, and, occasionally, assessments all wound up in these binders.

Once chairman, Welch committed to uprooting and removing this huge layer of bureaucracy that was paralyzing GE and holding the company back. He went on to fire more than a hundred thousand people. They called him "Neutron Jack." The buildings were fine, but there weren't any people in them. During his last ten years as chairman, he proceeded to rebuild the company on an entirely different basis. The new GE employed even more people than Welch originally fired, but the new management style was radically different.

Welch transformed GE from a bureaucracy into a far leaner company driven predominantly by a verbal vision and approach. Welch's style is exemplified by a specific area called "the Pit," located in GE's world education headquarters in Crotonville, New York. As he and others described it, every two weeks or so, Welch would visit the Pit to talk with large groups of managers—face-to-face, voice-to-voice, person-to-person. The only communication aids allowed were note cards. PowerPoint presentations, handouts, and other more typical management communication aids were banned. (He tells a great story about how he made a huge hiring mistake because the person's slide deck [this was in the days before PowerPoint] was so good. You'll have to read his book for that story.) Welch's goal was to get his managers to talk more about their businesses, challenges, issues, and approaches. He moved them away from elaborate, expensive, glossy, but superficial communication techniques.

One lesson I take from this is that a key to Welch's great success was converting GE from a culture of written bureaucracy, where everything is documented and stored, into a verbal culture of real-time decision making and action. Under Welch's leadership, your ability to explain yourself, debate, discuss, and decide, all pretty much on the spot, was a greater determinant of your continued success than whether or not the "notebook" was up-to-date.

Welch's approach was profoundly different from the standard of that time, one which, it would seem, only a very strong leader could execute. This approach brings with it a great insight about management and, therefore, informs one discipline of the trusted strategic advisor: the industrial world, the political world, the nonprofit world, the commercial world, all really run at a verbal velocity. Although we do use manuals, memos, slick A/V programs, and other kinds of high-technology communications tools, how we speak and orally direct each other is what gets things done. Even in this era of the Web, blogs, podcasts, and "high definition," it is through conversations between and among people that progress is ultimately achieved.

The trusted advisor has to be able to engage in fast-paced discussion in real time, which requires strong verbal skills, and do so in the territory of the executive, which is the future toward which the boss is steering the organization. You need verbal skills and a vision of the future; you need to be what I call a verbal visionary. I'll talk about the verbal skills first and then turn to the visionary aspect.

Advice on the Spot

What sets the external consultant apart most significantly from the internal advisor is the expectation of cogent, useful advice instantly, based on his or her extensive experience but very little information. More typically, with internal consultants, the process is to attend meetings, listen, ask questions, absorb the information, then leave to prepare a presentation, response, or outline of a plan for later discussion with the boss.

The problem with leaving to think about things is, of course, that if the issue requires more urgent attention or if the boss is focused on it now, strategic decision making will continue even if staff members intend to return to provide helpful information after a relatively short period of time.

One of the questions I frequently hear is, "Why, when the meeting is over, does the outside advisor get to go into the room with the boss and the lawyers, and I, who have worked here for nine or ten years, have to make an appointment?" This ability to give advice on the spot is one important reason. In terms of verbal skill, providing advice instantly is among the most crucial of disciplines for the trusted advisor. You can train yourself to do this. One way is to use the Three-Minute Drill, which I discuss in Chapter Nine. And later in this chapter, I'll provide some guidance in assessing your verbal skill.

Verbal skill is where the trusted strategic advisor's real power lies. What happened the last time someone presented the boss a plan to accomplish something—you remember, that beautiful two-inch-thick notebook, 150 pages, thirty-one tabs, and fifteen thousand well-chosen words? Was it actually read? Or did your boss simply put his hand on it, look the proposer in the eye, and say, "Show me what's in here and tell me how it's going to help us achieve our objectives"? One powerful element of visionary communication is to say less but make what is said more important; to write less but make it sayable, hearable, and brief. Refined, concentrated ideas and information, delivered directly and concisely, are what power up the relationship.

The Advisor's Verbal Toolbox

Leaders lead through their ability to verbalize the future, explain a direction, and describe a destination. The advisor also works in real time to help leaders lead in real time. Ideally the advisor's verbal skills should be models that the leader can learn from and imitate.

The advisor has six powerful verbal tools:

1. **Facts.** These are data and authoritative information, developed and verbally delivered appropriately and promptly.

2. **Stories.** These are structured verbal examples leaders use, which take audiences through ideas, concepts, problems, or situations vicariously, yet teach lessons, morals, or self-evident truths audiences can use to their benefit.

3. **Questions.** These are questions the leader can use to help engage others in discussions or conversations that move the organization forward. (It's also helpful to provide suggested answers.)

4. **Comparisons.** These could be part of a best-practice discussion or, more important, could mean sharing your perception of how another leader or leaders handled similar problems from different perspectives.

5. **Recommendations and options.** The currency of consulting and counseling is recommendations. Unless the way is absolutely crystal clear, it's often helpful to propose several options. Recommending options keeps clients and consultants engaged with each other. Recommending a useful series of actions along a timeline allows leaders to generate momentum and forward motion.

6. **Constructive confrontation.** At senior levels, ideas and recommendations are first debated and confronted before any consensus or collaboration process is considered. Just as lawyers are trained to be adversarial, operations executives are trained to make decisions only after a robust confrontation of all the options. Managers and leaders are taught that the way to get the best ideas is often through confrontation, the so-called clash of ideas, tough language, and argument. Most senior managers are trained to use this technique, because it reflects what was expected of them. Recognize that for really important decisions, the boss is going to let the debate rage for some time until emotions are exhausted, a few key ideas survive (along with their sponsors and advocates), and one or two key concepts or directions tend to emerge.

Be ready to rumble; get ready to roar. Get coaching if you need it. For many trusted advisors, this is the toughest test of all. Most staff advisors, whether from the inside or the outside, tend to be peacemakers, consensus builders, direction seekers, and momentum generators.

Assess Your Verbal Skill

If your company can afford it or if you can afford it, and perhaps even if you can't, have a professional assess your verbal skill; the understanding you will gain is highly beneficial and sometimes essential. Coaches by the hundreds, perhaps thousands, are available to do this. Let me suggest a very simple "do-it-yourself" method to get started. You can make it more elaborate thereafter if you feel it's necessary.

Buy a handheld microcassette tape or digital audio recorder. Audio voice notes and cell phone recorders will not work, as the recording time is too limited. Get in the habit of taking this machine to meetings and turning it on. (Be sure to tell everyone affected by what you are doing, and get their permission. Most people seem happy to help once they understand what you are doing.) Either alone or with someone you trust and respect, go back over these tapes and listen carefully to your conversations. Initially you may be put off by the sound of your voice, or surprised by hearing yourself in the context of a complete conversation. The goal is to look for speech patterns and vocal habits that spread confusion or get in the way of solutions, understanding, or the truth.

This technique is for private use. You make these recordings only for your own personal benefit, and presumably erase them for continuous reuse in the recording device. Initially this practice may inhibit conversation, but if you use this technique regularly, others will come to see it simply as a part of what you do, especially if you report on the progress you are making and what you are learning about yourself.

Another option is to record meetings where you make presentations. These presentations can be transcribed and sent to other managers. You use the audiotapes to critique your performance.

You will become more discerning about what you talk about and how you say things. If you listen carefully, one of the great revelations will be of why people misunderstand you or do things differently than you expect based on the instructions you thought you gave. You begin to discern the difference between what you say and what your audience hears.

In my experience, when a person uses this approach carefully and regularly, his or her verbal skills improve noticeably. Others will notice and comment about it. During my lectures, I estimate that fewer than one in a hundred people actually take this suggestion and carry it out, but many of those who do contact me to talk about how powerfully they were helped by this process.

One CEO's administrative assistant told me she had to browbeat him for months to begin doing this. Her boss finally gave in and took one of these devices to his Friday direct reports meeting. As he told me the story afterward, these meetings always produced additional meetings as a result of the subjects covered. They were held early on Fridays so that everything could be wrapped up before the weekend. This way, Mondays would begin with a fresh perspective, plan, and action—pretty smart.

The CEO related to me that within thirty-five minutes after the recorded meeting ended, three people made appointments to meet with him on Monday. Having listened to the tape, he said that as soon as he saw the appointments on his calendar, he knew exactly why they were there. During the meeting, the CEO had told one of the people who had offered a suggestion that he "didn't think the idea was workable." As the CEO thought about it afterward, it was obvious to him that these individuals had scheduled meetings to "find out what the heck I was talking about." The CEO now knew that his comments were unintelligible and confusing.

Regularly listen to yourself talk. This is part of the discipline of attaining verbal skill. You will improve; you will maintain a better sense of on-the-spot verbal planning as you talk. But most important, those around you will benefit from your clearer, more concise and constructive conversation.

Get Coaching

If your problems are more serious, if you are apprehensive or fearful, or if those you respect have suggested that you need help in this area, there are many good coaches who can assist you. Most public relations firms have individuals who are skilled in coach-ing for public performance and news interviews. You can pick up almost any current book on speaking skills and benefit from the one or two, maybe more, ideas that will immediately stand out and that you can implement. But the most successful way of all beyond the self-assessment is to locate and use a presentation coach to help you develop and enhance your verbal skill. The following are my favorite presentation skills books of all time:

> *Get to the Point: How to Say What You Mean and Get What You Want*, by Karen Berg and Andrew Gilman (Bantam Books, 1989)
>
> *The Articulate Executive: Learn to Look, Act, and Sound Like a Leader*, by Granville N. Toogood (McGraw-Hill, 1996)
>
> *The Inspired Executive: The Art of Leadership in the Age of Knowledge*, by Granville N. Toogood (Carroll & Graf, 1997)

Yes, these books have been around a while, but they are simply excellent.

Being Visionary

The greatest responsibility of leadership is identifying the vision or destinations toward which the organization is moving. The abil-ity to do this is part of the genius all leaders must bring. Some are better at it than others, but all have to have a larger sense of where we are going than anyone else in the organization. The trusted strategic advisor is a crucial partner in that visu-alization of an organization's destiny. His or her ability to help formulate, organize, structure, and then verbalize this vision is extraordinarily valuable.

Let's delve into the concepts of vision and of being a visionary, and tie the two concepts together. I define *vision* as a meaningful, useful, positive goal that many can willingly contribute to achiev-ing. When corporate vision programs fail to reflect this definition, people ignore them because vague visions are simply irrelevant.

They often are framed in rigid, jargon-laden terms like "sense of urgency," "hypereffectiveness," or "beyond wow." Even the boss fails to follow them. This is why many corporate vision statements end up as just nice plaques that hang on the wall.

A *visionary* is an optimistic individual who can get others to focus on the future or on some meaningful, useful, positive goals, which those others willingly contribute to achieving. A verbally visionary advisor is someone capable, through the use of sensibly applied speech power, of moving leaders to focus on the future and to help them better interpret their vision.

A true verbal visionary is also quite strategic. A strategist is one who is able to analyze effectively, forecast pragmatically, focus realistically on issues and problems, candidly interpret events and ideas and their impact, and generate ethically and morally appropriate options for decision making, action, and progress. All top executives are the key strategists in their organization.

Very few managers or senior executives are verbal visionaries. Some will resist the notion of being visionary because they feel that their approaches are, at the very least, pragmatic and useful. They may want to resist overstating their face value. Nonvisionaries are people who follow rigid rules, people who are so emotionally attached to personal concepts and ideas that they have difficulty adapting what they are doing to the needs of others. Nonvisionaries have little tolerance for anything outside the patterns of their own beliefs.

A Verbal Visionary Understands What People Value

A verbal visionary understands people and what people value. *Values*, in my experience, are protective personal beliefs; they are almost impossible to change because they serve as such powerful entitlement mechanisms. I'm talking about issues related to health and safety, environmental protection, quality of life, work and employment, and other truly personal values, such as honesty and integrity. Organizations don't impose a value system on people; people bring their values into organizations. Wherever these value systems agree, there will be values-driven behavior. Where these values conflict, it is the individual's values—in other words, their personal protective beliefs—that will prevail and determine behavior and results.

A Verbal Visionary Is a Trustworthy Person

Remember, trust is the absence of fear. You trust someone because you feel safe around him or her. You are confident that the person won't hurt you or is unlikely to hurt you. A trustworthy person has all the attributes discussed in the previous chapter: candor, credibility, competence, integrity, and loyalty.

What Does a Verbal Visionary Do?

First of all, a verbal visionary is a *counselor*. An effective counselor is a pragmatist, a truth seeker and candid truth teller, a storyteller, and an inspiration and motivator to others. As a pragmatist, the verbal visionary defines reality in terms of what will actually happen. In some ways you could say that a pragmatist is the opposite of a dreamer. Most pragmatists have the sense of reality necessary to help bring dreams to life. A pragmatist is someone who gets the getable, knows the knowable, does the doable, and achieves the achievable.

A counselor is a truth coach, someone who avoids the trap of believing in narrow truths that ultimately satisfy no one. If truth seems difficult to find, the counselor helps build bridges to that truth, the whole truth.

Truth is complex. In my view, it is helpful to define truth as 15 percent fact and 85 percent perception and emotion. The visionary counselor helps illuminate various points of reference so that the truth and the various perspectives that truth represents can be more clearly understood. For example, let's say four individuals witness a car accident at an intersection, each from a different corner. An experienced traffic officer interviews these four witnesses. Two witnesses agree on the number of vehicles involved; the other two do not. A different pair agrees on the weather conditions; the other two have different views. A different pair agrees on the condition of the traffic signal at the intersection; the other two disagree. Beyond that, all their observations conflict. Why? It is because each individual witnessed the accident from a different point of reference. Yet the underlying conflicting information presented by each witness is the truth as he or she saw it. That's why truth can be complicated. Truth requires understanding and interpretation. Truth requires recognition of the viewer's point of reference.

A verbal visionary is usually very candid. As I've stated elsewhere, candor is truth told with an attitude. It is truth with meaning and with insight. A person who is candid is a person who demystifies, who decodes, who deciphers, who de-emotionalizes, and who demythologizes complex ideas and truths. A verbal visionary candidly interprets and clarifies information in ways that are obviously helpful, and avoids being self-serving.

Be a Storyteller

A counselor is also a storyteller, and storytelling is among the most powerful verbal techniques in any culture, especially for leaders. Stories are one of the verbal visionary's most effective tools, yet even very experienced communicators often have trouble telling stories.

Successful stories are generally told in plain, fundamentally positive language. They are about people, animals, living systems, or some combination of the three. They are relatively brief and have a recognizable beginning, middle, and end. Most important, stories have a moral, a lesson, what I call a self-evident truth or reason for being told that is immediately recognizable to the listener. Stories help us learn from our own perspective, our own point of reference. We are motivated by the stories of others, but from our own individual perspectives. Each of us can be changed by the same story, but in different ways.

There are all kinds of stories: stories that make you cry, stories that make you laugh, stories that make you think, stories that grab your belly and squeeze it, stories that humiliate or make you feel ashamed. The best stories are usually very memorable (which I discuss further in the next section).

Stories have impact because they answer the questions we would ask, if we could: What happened? What was it like? How did it feel? Often it is the opportunity to obtain answers to important questions that draws us to a storyteller, or to a verbal visionary. Stories often clarify the confusion of our struggles and the chaos of daily life. Stories move us, exerting amazing motivational and emotional energy. Those who tell stories well have great impact.

Every leader needs to use stories as one of his or her principal teaching, coaching, and disciplinary tools. *Reader's Digest* can help. (Forty-three years ago, my mother-in-law began sending me *Reader's Digest* every month. I love that magazine because it is full of stories that virtually anyone can understand, learn from, or tell.) Here's an example.

I was going to speak before a large audience of government communicators, and I was hunting for a relevant story. As I am a former government communicator, which the audience members all knew, I had a bit of latitude about the kind of story I could tell. I came across a story in *Reader's Digest* that was absolutely perfect. It talked about both government communication and working for government. Here's the story.

A man was sitting on his porch on a warm, sunny day, looking down the street and watching a city street crew working on the boulevards in front of houses. The truck would pull up in front of each lot; the passenger would hop out and dig a hole in the boulevard, then get back in the truck. A couple of minutes would pass and then the driver would get out, fill in the hole, pat the dirt down, get back in the truck, and drive on to the next house. This behavior, of course, puzzled the observer. When they got to his front yard, he hopped off the porch, walked down to the truck, banged on the window, and asked what these guys were doing. The driver rolled down the window and said, "We're planting trees." The neighbor asked, "What do you mean planting trees? Your buddy gets out and digs a hole, then you get out of the truck and fill it in, and you drive on to the next house. Where are the trees you're planting?" "Oh," said the driver, "the guy who actually plants trees is out sick today."

My question to the audience was, "How many holes are being filled in at your office today because you're at this meeting listening to me?"

Be Memorable

Intend to be remembered. It is a skill. Take the time to learn. Invest the effort. Being memorable is up to you. Who will remember you unless you help them. Fail to be rememorable, and you're wasting someone's time.

What do I mean by being intentionally memorable? Say and do things that you know people will want to remember—special words or phrases, or stories that are particularly memorable. One example is verbally shaping ideas so as to be easily quoted by others. Do people quote you? Talk in memorable language. Most leaders are destiny driven. They have a picture or sense of their future. Compare your own sense of destiny to the sense of destiny of those you want to help. People who lead think and strategize constantly about their own future, their goals, their ambitions, and their fears. It helps you to have reflected on these questions yourself—both from your own perspective and the perspective of those you are advising. The conversations that can develop from this thinking are often very powerful, very personal, and very meaningful to both of you.

Being intentionally memorable means telling stories well enough so that your stories are carried on and told by others, often without any attribution to you. Your stories are so useful, so helpful, so illustrative, so interesting that the people who hear them will simply adopt them as a part of their own behavior and way of influencing others. Use stories that help define how listeners achieve their objectives.

Simply put, to be memorable, you have to act in ways that will be remembered—you have to do or say memorable things on purpose.

Be Inspirational

A verbal visionary is also a motivator and an inspiration. Helping leaders be inspirational is quite often one of the expectations of the coach and counselor. How do you inspire? How does one become a motivator? Are there techniques a person can learn to do this? Yes. You can learn and practice modeling your skills and sharing what you say in ways that are motivational and inspirational. We learn to inspire others by being inspired by others. Developing this ability requires that you pay attention to what moves other people and what other people want. You have to want to help others achieve their goals before you achieve yours; or, better yet, adopt their goals and aspirations as your own so that you'll achieve them together.

The people who are good at this are those who truly want to have an impact on others and who really work at being good at having an impact—generally a positive impact—on other people. The kind of visionary you're likely to be will be reflected in those you see around you or who themselves are visionaries or who have enormous influence on many people. Study what they do; pay attention to how they motivate and how they inspire. One of the best ways to learn this skill is to have those who are already good at it around you or the leader you serve.

What inspires you? What moves you forward? A powerful, honest personal commitment to others is required. If those around you fail to inspire you or others, it is time to move on and find those who do.

CEOs implicitly choose to be inspirational when they decide to take the job. That's because inspiring and motivating are essential to the role. For most other managerial roles, the choice to be inspirational is optional.

My mother-in-law, Ruth, is probably among the most inspirational people I've known in my life. She has this knack for listening to you speak and then coming up with an absolutely perfect response. I've often felt that she should write a book of her own about the wisdom she has. One time we were talking about another relative, who was being given a hard time by both his family and his pastor. Among other things, this relative had a drinking problem. Ruth's analysis was, "More often than not, you find far greater compassion in a bar than in a church." Ruth's presence and delivery made the comment very memorable.

Be Thoughtful

A verbal visionary is also thoughtful. My understanding of a thoughtful person is that he or she does four critical things routinely.

First, the thoughtful person uses verbal contrast analysis. In other words, when a thoughtful person analyzes a situation, problem, issue, or opportunity, he or she is able to draw a verbal contrast between good and bad, bland and colorful, the emotional and the factual. This is what people are looking for in terms of help. Useful simplification leads to verbal contrasts, which inspire understanding.

Second, a thoughtful person asks good questions—questions intended to build understanding rather than to attack, demean, diminish, minimize, or bully. Good questions generate answers that help everyone within earshot.

Third, a thoughtful person is a constructive skeptic. This means that in the absence of obviously conclusive evidence, the person constructively analyzes ideas, purposes, and intentions.

He or she usefully dissects imperfect ideas, thoughtfully examines them, then discusses them—again with a focus on learning, on illustrating, on understanding, on gaining insight. It's the triggering of insight that really leads to what we perceive as wisdom.

Fourth, a thoughtful person states the obvious at every turn. Stating the obvious simplifies so many things very, very rapidly.

My favorite story about stating the obvious comes from a Sherlock Holmes novel, *The Hound of the Baskervilles*. In one scene, Holmes and Watson are tracking a murderer across a Scottish moor, and they are forced to camp out overnight. Early in the morning, Holmes wakes Watson and says, "Watson, Watson, look at those stars. What do they mean?" Watson replies, "Well, Holmes, horologically it's about three o'clock in the morning; meteorologically, it's likely to be a pleasant day; theologically, God is in his heavens and his minions are resting comfortably in their beds. What does it mean to you?"

"Watson, you idiot," said Holmes. "Someone has stolen our tent!" A funny but powerful story.

As a thoughtful person, you state the obvious and *see* the obvious, often hidden in plain sight. Being thoughtful can allow you to simplify complex ideas and concepts in a dramatic and positive way, and doing so can snap on that little light in your brain—that powerful, momentary illumination of understanding or insight. You suddenly "see" what was hidden there before, even if it is blindingly obvious. Perhaps you've heard of Occam's razor, named after the fourteenth-century mathematician. To paraphrase the concept: assuming that most other factors are equal, the simplest explanation is likely to be the correct one. It is often also the most sensible. The ability to focus and to wield Occam's razor is one of the arts of the verbal visionary.

Individuals who are thoughtful can be very insightful. To me, people who are insightful are those who can extract intuitively clear ideas from existing complex situations or information. We listen to them or read their words, and we feel or instinctively know that they are right or that what they are saying has inherent value. They open new doors or pathways by detecting useful information, clarifying misunderstanding, distilling simplicity from complex ideas and information. Insightful people can creatively illustrate a problem, idea, or issue; develop a quick, concise, and powerful analysis that brings the listener or reader a sense of relief, surprise, clarity, or closure.

Be Ethical

A verbal visionary is ethical—that is, principled. A visionary lives by a set of rules and personal command behaviors (self-imposed virtues) that all of us recognize as predominantly in the interest of others. A verbal visionary is an advocate for honorable action, an individual who is morally assertive (minus the religious fervor) and infused with a passion for the right behaviors, ideas, and actions at every turn, especially in the face of ethical dilemmas.

Be a Coach and Mentor

A verbal visionary is a coach, someone who is committed to helping others more than helping himself or herself. The visionary coaches by usefully interpreting events and ideas, illustrating new approaches, and exemplifying the very behaviors, ideas, and concepts that will be most helpful to the individual being coached. A coach can forecast patterns, predict with a great deal of accuracy how organizations and individuals behave, and prepare everyone for the unintended consequences of his or her actions.

A verbal visionary is also a mentor. A mentor is someone who starts from the other person's point of view or reference—always. A mentor is someone who helps others focus on goals that are worth achieving, who helps leaders build followership, who helps others see options they can't see for themselves. A mentor is someone who is outcome focused. By that I mean someone who's always focused forward, focused on the future.

These are also key elements in the definition of a strategist. A strategist is someone who is focused on what is going to happen, what might happen, and what is possible; someone who knows the lessons of the past but isn't always looking backward, trying to reanalyze, relive, redefine, or reinterpret history—the old should'a, would'a, could'a analysis that helps no one.

Be Virtuous

Another ingredient of the visionary is virtue. What are your virtues, those forces in your life that help you stay focused on achieving good, useful, important, and powerful things? Those personal habits that keep you out of trouble?

One of the most famous lists of virtues was written by Benjamin Franklin. He describes them extensively in *Poor Richard's Almanac*, and his notes and records exist to this day. He began with twelve. Each was printed on a separate page in a diary he kept. He would pick one and work on it for a month, then select another, month by month throughout the year. His original twelve virtues were temperance, silence, order, resolution, frugality, industry, sincerity, justice, moderation, cleanliness, tranquillity, and chastity. He maintained this practice for more than fifty years. An interesting side story about Franklin's list of virtues was that sometime later in his life, as he became world famous, some of his friends in Philadelphia pointed out to him that he was becoming a bit insufferable. A couple of them even suggested that he needed to add another virtue to his famous list of twelve. That thirteenth virtue was humility. Franklin added it and worked on it as he did the others.

Consider using Franklin's approach. A verbal visionary lives and works his or her principles, values, aspirations, virtues, and vision every day. What are your virtues, those personal habits that you need to cultivate, practice, and exercise such that they maintain their impact on your life? When one is clear on these things, other people can tell. The clarity of these ideas permeates your conduct and your discourse.

You will find that those who come to rely on you as a verbal visionary will expect you to express and discuss your principles, your aspirations, the foundation of your beliefs, where your thinking comes from, how you arrive at your own internal destinations. Anyone can offer advice and make guesses with no particular basis of fact or knowledge. Being a verbal visionary means that you understand your self-concepts deeply and share them as a method of reinforcing the value and depth of your advice. This approach to your life helps you guide important people in their lives. They will notice and listen because the way forward is not always clear. Their responsibilities require that they consult trusted strategic advisors to help chart the way ahead.

How Do You Become a Verbal Visionary?

So how do you begin to become a verbal visionary (or know that you are one already)? What are the attributes of a verbal visionary? Your analysis begins by asking yourself some very difficult but important questions. You strive to understand yourself. For example:

- What do you believe? What are the truths of your life? Write these beliefs down. Even though what you believe rarely changes, writing them down and saying them out loud is a surprisingly powerful personal experience, I promise.
- Who are you? How do you describe yourself? Say it out loud. Write it down.
- What are your personal limitations? Are there things you can't do or won't do?
- What are your aspirations? Who, what, where do you want to be? Write them down.
- What are your principles? What are the parameters of your life? Write them down.
- What is your daily goal or reason for doing what you do?
- What do you see as your destiny? Do you have an inner sense of where you are going? What do you want to leave behind? What will people remember about you? What do you want people to remember about you? Write it down in one hundred words; say it out loud.

Talk these ideas through. Say them out loud. Get in the habit of asking important questions about yourself. This is not an exercise in vanity; rather, actively contemplating these questions outside of your inner voice will have a powerful transformative effect on you. Talking about them out loud helps you talk about them in a variety of circumstances. Refine and test your answers against your experience and expectations of yourself. Be prepared to talk about them in the context of those you council. Leaders do this automatically. They can usually discuss all these topics because their life experience and expectations are the basis for their leadership.

We are talking about your bringing an enhanced degree of personal authenticity and presence—your self-understanding, your belief system, those things that motivate you—to your ability to explain and discuss your advice, your vision, and the vision you have for others. It is this ability that builds respect. You have the *respect* of those you advise when they honor you and hold you and your ideas in high regard. You'll know you are influencing their lives. If you don't feel this, you simply are not doing it. You are in fact wasting someone's time.

Next, you also have to strive to understand the beliefs of those who rely on you. These are the questions to ask of or about them:

- What do they believe?
- What motivates them?
- How can you help them achieve their objectives?
- What about their beliefs and ideas is obviously true?
- What is obviously untrue? Silly, naive, or stupid?
- Where or how can you make the most important contribution for those individuals, from their perspective?

Write this information down, too. Then take another step. Contrast your beliefs directly with their beliefs. Contrast what motivates them with what motivates you. Contrast how they believe they can use your help with how you believe you can help them. Contrast what's true to them with what's true to you. Contrast what's silly to them with what's silly to you. What is the most important contribution you can make for them, from their perspective?

Think of a contrast analysis as a single sheet of paper with a line drawn from top to bottom down the center. Write your beliefs and aspirations on the left side of the sheet, and the boss's aspirations and expectations on the right. Do they match? How different are they? Contrast analysis is a simple, extremely efficient and effective talking, teaching, and personal learning tool.

How Will You Know If You Have Become a Verbal Visionary?

One of the most satisfying and powerful aspects of being a verbal visionary is knowing that the advice you offer and your ability to explore important personal ideas and concepts are genuinely helpful in terms of the leaders' goals and objectives, personal beliefs and motivations, sense of reality, and priority of ideas. Leaders tell you and others how you've helped them, and your insights become evident in their decisions, actions, beliefs, and strategies.

Can you sense the power of a verbal visionary? Can you become one? If this concept seems to be "out there" for you, my suggestion is that you rethink just how much you want to be in that inner circle. How much can you actually contribute?

You have role models in your life who can help you refine your verbal visionary skills—memorable people, whether they're relatives, friends, teachers, famous, or not famous people. You remember them predominantly because of what you saw or heard, learned or felt, and how they affected you.

Your greatest role model of all may be the leader you counsel or want to counsel, just down the hall.

If you want to take up the challenge of becoming a verbal visionary, here's a personal checklist you can use to assess your progress and practices:

- Do I act and speak in other people's best interests all the time?
- Am I a mentor? Can I be outcome focused?
- Am I quoted by those I respect and those who seek my help?
- Do people take action based on what I say? Do people talk about me as being a person of vision, as an extraordinarily positive, helpful person?
- Do I feel like a verbal visionary? Can I tell when I'm actually moving people to action and helping them find the emotional energy to benefit themselves?
- Can I describe my own sense of destiny, my principles, my beliefs, my limits, my virtues?
- Can I systematically go after the truth first? Am I a pragmatist?

The more yes answers, the more likely it is that you are well on your way to becoming or being a verbal visionary.

6

DEVELOP A MANAGEMENT PERSPECTIVE

Chapter Outline

Admission to the Inner Circle

Commit Yourself to Management's Team

Ask Managerially Relevant Questions First

Be Ready with Answers

Why Bosses Sometimes Bypass Staff

Whining Turns Bosses Off

Say Things That Matter

Questions to Consider

People in staff functions tend to believe that their recommendations, big ideas, or silver bullets will save the day for management. In reality, silver bullets, big ideas, and brilliant strategies are extraordinarily rare. Those in operations learn relatively quickly that most progress is actually made incrementally, often following established patterns of thinking, experience, and scientific or at least rigorous exploration and study, with a hint of intuition and strategic thinking. Most solutions arrive by accident and chance, as the by-products of some incremental approach.

The trusted strategic advisor develops the discipline of understanding the management perspective and learns to use management points of reference more than the jargon of his or her staff function. To be invited into the inner circle, you have to focus on and sound like you know what matters there.

Admission to the Inner Circle

Despite the fact that many senior and top managers are loners or, at the very least, selective about who gets near them, there almost always is an inner circle. Those who populate this special group can be surprising. The variety can range from a person in the shipping department to the president of the United States. What does the shipping clerk have in common with the president? It's all in the eyes, emotions, and needs of the beholder—the CEO. One thing these advisors all seem to have in common is the ability to offer the leader suggestions and options from which the leader can then fashion a solution or process to reach a decision.

An early client of mine, we'll call him Wilson, was the head of corporate security for one of America's largest companies. He was, in that position, an extraordinarily sought-after advisor to the CEO and senior management. He told me that he came to the attention of the CEO when he had first joined the company from the FBI and had to be a stand-in for his boss at a social gathering. When the time came for someone to organize the presentations, he stepped forward. In the process of carrying out this assignment, he told a couple of stories and, he told me with a straight face, sang a short song. As it turned out, the CEO was quite taken by this extemporaneous ability and began inviting him to other meetings. Wilson's stepping forward in this circumstance brought him unexpected, important attention from people who mattered. With what started out as a unique, chance circumstance, he was able to build a career based on powerful relationships with very senior people, involving some of the most important issues the corporation was facing in the United States and globally.

Although this may sound like a cliché, your mind-set has to be one of putting yourself into the manager's shoes, both operationally and nonoperationally. Among other things, this means being conversant with current business plans and key business strategies, and having some familiarity with the metrics of the business. These make up the boss's world. If you want to be there, you must know the terrain. The discipline of maintaining a management perspective is the discipline of reducing exuberance and instilling a measured, more thoughtful and incremental approach to making recommendations and suggestions.

Familiarity with key or crucial business issues is essential. These are the questions, roadblocks, barriers, and threats that can confound even the most enlightened management and the most aggressive and cohesive organization. If the greatest threat has to do with people's attitudes, become good at understanding these circumstances. If the problems involve markets and marketing strategy, find a way to become more strategic and knowledgeable in these areas. It's these key issues that often derail the most well-thought-out plans. What keeps your boss awake at night? What's left to be done from last week? In many respects, until these issues are addressed, nothing else matters.

Define your staff function in management terms rather than just in the terms of staff expertise. The staff person's failure to align the activities and goals of his or her function with management objectives is often the reason that person is considered less important to the operations team. Here's an example using the public relations function, although it applies equally well to other functions, such as legal, HR, marketing, finance, strategic planning, compliance, or IT. According to my conversations with management,

- PR staff are rarely thought of as having sufficient knowledge or practical experience to contribute significant operational solutions.
- PR recommendations can come across as "public relations speak" dressed up in the business vocabulary of the moment. When the rhetoric is stripped away, there are very few operational solutions.
- Management has learned the lesson—from PR staff—that it is far easier to take an operating person and make him or her

into a public affairs or PR practitioner than it is to transform a public affairs or PR practitioner into an effective operating executive.

- The PR focus is too often on defending the function, the media, even the words "public relations." One frustrated executive told me, "I wish they'd be as passionate about the needs I have around here as they are about defining and defending what the news media does and needs."

I'm sure you can come up with a similar list of management perceptions about your particular function.

The example I gave in Chapter Three provides another way to look at using management language. You'll recall that when a communications firm was acquired by a large international consulting firm, its people undertook to reinvent the language they used to describe their services. "Internal communications" became "employee loyalty building," "brainstorming and ideation" became "strategic planning," "communication audit" became "operational review and analysis," and so on. Notice the much more powerful "feeling" these descriptions inspire. They also contain words managers tend to understand.

The staff practitioner may resent having to translate the descriptions of the professional functions and services, skills, and techniques about which he or she cares so deeply into the more turgid language of management. It is simply a practical reality that to be understood by management, the staff expert or outside advisor must use management terms and actually execute in the management environment.

Commit Yourself to Management's Team

One of the more challenging issues you must face as a trusted advisor is the realization that to be inside, to be close by, to have that close relationship, you have to do more than just want to be there or feel that by virtue of your position you have some inherent right to be there. You have to take an emotional and psychological leap forward and put yourself as directly as possible into the environment and mentality of this person you are advising. How do you put yourself in the boss's shoes? One useful way is to be guided by a series of professional commitment statements. You can be comfortable with these statements because they help you get to where you need to be and reveal your commitment to understand, support, and work with management from its perspective.

- Service is why I'm here—to protect, serve, advise, and represent the boss rather than my department or function.
- It is top management's vision and values that drive the organization day to day and over the long term rather than my personal agenda. As a trusted advisor, I always focus on the needs of the person being advised.
- The coaching process begins by understanding what the boss's problems are. My job is to set my problems aside.
- My job is to help management solve, control, contain, preempt, and counteract management problems. I'm there to ensure success, even if that success makes things difficult for my department. I'll suggest solutions that may be good for the organization even if my function has to take a hit.
- Building followership is a key strategy and management goal. I am a loyal follower, and I can help build more.
- Expressing solutions in management language, rather than in staff language, helps top executives feel mentored and motivated. This is one of the key reasons trusted advisors are around—to mentor, motivate, and inspire.
- I always strive to make positive suggestions. I will forgo criticism. Criticism is negative and distracting, and it creates enemies and critics.
- The boss knows and listens to me because I am a professional and a trusted strategic advisor. My work and attitude and the strength of my advice are the justifications of my value every day.

Ask Managerially Relevant Questions First

One of the most important roles of the trusted strategic advisor is to ask constructive questions that help broaden understanding and move processes and decision making to the next level.

Too often, staff tend to use questions as a means of demeaning, maligning, or murdering the advice of other advisors. Here are some examples:

"Why am I just hearing about this now?"

"Where is the justification for this request?"

"Where did this come from? How many have done it successfully before?"

"Why wasn't this circulated earlier for more thorough consideration?"

"Shouldn't they have gone through IT, finance, or strategic planning first?"

"Who authorized this much off-the-reservation effort?"

I often refer to this as death by question. If this is your approach, you need to end it immediately. Insults and needlessly combative negative opposition through questioning are always remembered. What goes around will come back around. Negativity creates critics, victims, and adversaries. These individuals persist forever and resurface at the worst possible times.

Even though you learn that the senior executive environment is fairly combative and confrontational, your goal has to be to preserve loyalty, develop constructive next steps, and reduce the production of critics.

Managerially relevant questions are designed to foster discussion and the productive exploration of ideas. They bring more critically essential understanding to the boss. Here's a list of those kinds of questions, which are almost always relevant:

- How does the current situation affect strategy?
- Which management mistakes change the strategy?
- How can we gain employee commitment to the changing circumstances that are causing the problem we're now facing?
- What strategies are available to us to keep shareholder interest aligned with our goals?
- Can management make the tough decisions and act quickly enough to turn a problem situation into an opportunity or at least into a mitigative circumstance?
- What resources can management allocate now to deal with the issues at hand or to resolve matters in ways that align with our strategy?
- What have peer companies done in similar circumstances? Do we care?
- How will the present circumstances affect our ability to research and develop new products, services, and ideas?
- Is this a situation that requires adaptation or dramatic shifts and changes?
- What nonfinancial factors are of greatest concern? What about the direct financial factors?
- Will customer satisfaction be adversely affected?
- What are the compliance and ethical implications of the current situation, and what remedial steps will be necessary?
- Have any rules, regulations, or laws been bent, broken, or compromised?

If many of these questions seem confrontational, it's because they are. This is part of your role as a constructive skeptic, as a productive, constructive questioner. It is a part of the rough-and-tumble world of a top strategic advisor. Get comfortable asking questions that have a constructively confrontational (rather than negative) tone. Every idea can be subject to a clash of thinking and alternative comparisons.

Be Ready with Answers

In terms of operations, asking questions is an excellent method for triggering incremental improvement. However, the job of the trusted strategic advisor is to simultaneously develop answers and answer strategies.

There are a variety of circumstances senior executives find themselves facing that require dramatic and intensive question-and-answer preparation. These would include testimony before governmental bodies, private agencies, employees, shareholders, and directors; presentations to business groups or in academic environments; the presentation of dramatic new ideas, theories, or strategies; and dealing with angry neighbors and highly emotional situations.

From my perspective, every time there is the possibility that questions will be asked, the advisor's role is to be prepared, in advance, with answer component recommendations as well as answer reasoning advice. Perhaps the most extreme organized form of this preparation—the "murder board"—was invented by the U.S. military. The murder board is a committee of questioners set up to help prepare someone for a difficult oral examination or other circumstance. This technique is used in academia as well, and in various other high-profile circumstances where the stakes are truly high for an executive or leader and the public answering of questions is a key ingredient.

One of the more common environments in which this murder board technique is encountered is in preparing CEOs for their presentation to shareholders at the annual meeting. During the final stages of presentation preparation, the CEO meets with rather large groups of advisors, technical and operations experts from inside and outside the organization. Each is there to listen for specific elements in the CEO's presentation and then to ask the CEO important, serious, hard, and often confrontational questions. These questions can be about the content, the commentary, the philosophy, or the strategy illustrated in the presentation, or even about the propriety of raising certain questions or issues.

This is one of the most important arenas for the trusted advisor's assistance. As the CEO develops answers for these questions, the trusted advisor is there coaching, suggesting, recommending, and creating best-answer and best-explanation options.

Why Bosses Sometimes Bypass Staff

Bosses seek many voices and viewpoints. It's a way to build the evidence necessary for better decision making and for identifying additional action options. But there is also a darker reason. Virtually every top executive I have counseled in my career can comment instantly on why they feel that internal staff or the current group of advisors falls short. These comments should stimulate some serious thinking by those who work internally and seek to be trusted at the top.

"Staff's first inclination is to teach their function." Lawyers love the law, finance people love the deal, HR people defend employees, and PR people tend to worry about the news media. Unless your staff function point is unique, insightful, or unusually different, you are better off focusing on the management issues at hand.

"Staff people constantly seem to be seeking approval for their behaviors, and confirmation of the value they bring and the value of their function." It may be tone of voice or choice of words that indicate the boss is being less than supportive or has in fact failed to recognize past contributions. The insight of this discussion, of course, is that almost anything about yesterday has very little interest for the boss. Talk in terms of tomorrow; be known as someone who is facing forward, all the time.

"Staff people fail to demonstrate that they understand either the business or the key issues the business faces." This problem comes from not knowing the boss better and consequently those issues, problems, and challenges that keep this top person either irritated or energized. You have to talk about both what matters and what's relevant in the context of the business, circumstance, or issue. It's very wise to apply these same lessons to the needs of senior staff and operational people around the CEO or senior leader as well.

"Staff people speak a language the boss neither needs nor cares to learn." This is very close to the first comment about how staff people tend to define everything in terms of their staff function and staff priorities. But this comment is mostly about staff's using words that are neither useful for management nor focused on the future. Yes, you can use words from your functional area or specialty, but they need to be couched and translated into terms managers can work with, understand, and be inspired by.

"Staff people focus on the unimportant." The question I find myself asking most frequently in any discussion is, "Does this really matter?" The topic of discussion may in fact matter, but there needs to be a constant checking and elimination process to stay focused on that magical, powerful 5 percent that really does matter.

"Staff people constantly take up management's time, telling us things we already know." From staff's perspective, management people may not necessarily know a lot about what they're getting into, what they're caught up in, or where they're headed. In most of the conversations I am a witness to, there is a fair amount of staff educational language that goes on before an advisor actually gets to the point about what he or she is recommending, suggesting, or illustrating. My feeling always is, get to the point first. Minimize the amount of education required, and do the educating after you've made your point. Give top people credit for knowing things beyond what you know. More important, they need to know far less than you think to make decisions.

"PR people would rather alienate the boss than a reporter." This is a special caveat for the communications advisor. Almost all executives feel this way; I often refer to this as paycheck confusion. That is, the boss wonders if the communicator actually remembers where the paycheck comes from. "Do they work for me or for the local newspaper today?" is something I hear from time to time.

The HR advisor is criticized because she is not tough enough. HR is "too soft on people." The lawyer is criticized for acting as if he runs the business.

IT people nearly always question another person's competence or qualifications rather than change their approach or challenge their own thinking and methods.

"Staff people may write well, but their verbal skills are undisciplined and unfocused, and fail to provide information management can act on." "They have trouble getting to the point." There's something about staff advice that appears to be based far more on emotion and a kind of staff-driven logic than on facts, data, in-depth knowledge, or experience. This kind of criticism among bosses can be toxic to advisor relationships. If you advise a senior executive to do something "because you believe in your heart that it's the right thing to do," the executive will also look outside to someone else for a more experienced, justifiable, or rational viewpoint.

Although it may seem hard to believe, what is desired, required, and needed at the top is the truth rather than the varnish. If you genuinely question whether your boss is looking for the truth, why do you stay?

Whining Turns Bosses Off

The most significant single reason senior executives and CEOs mention to me for why they have difficulty working with staff functions in their own organizations is the amount of whining in which these functions indulge. Staff people whine about budgets, about each other, about the direction things are going, about not being consulted, about the fact that they could have given better information sooner if only they had been included in the discussions. What is fascinating, and a little scary, is that while CEOs and other executives hold these perceptions, staff people have their own whiney excuses for not being in the loop and not being consulted (and if they had been, the organization and its leadership should'a, would'a, could'a done better than it did).

Here are the whiniest excuses I hear from staff functions. By the way, bosses know staff say these things, and it subtracts from the staff's credibility and value as members of the team.

- They don't understand the power of my function.
- They don't appreciate the function.
- They always consult the lawyers and management consultants before they talk to us, and we get stuck cleaning up even bigger messes.
- The CEO is pretty bright, but has blind spots and prejudices that will get us into trouble one of these days.
- We could have told them that this was going to happen, but we couldn't break through the silos and the arrogant mentality that "management is smart enough to handle anything."
- If I got more face time, things would be different.
- Why do they still blame us, but won't talk to us or allow us to have early input?
- Everything is so last minute. Management doesn't follow its own plan (or even have a plan).

Let me offer some suggestions about other changes you will need to make in your strategy to develop a management perspective.

This bears repeating: learn, talk about, and teach things that matter to management. Practice and use everything else in the privacy of your functional staff activities. To matter to management, you need to provide information and insights that go beyond what the boss or your advisee already knows. After all, if all you do is provide information about stuff they know or have already decided, of what value is it? If all you have to offer are the plati-tudes of your staff function and the simple stuff, you are unlikely to be invited back on a regular basis.

Mattering to management also means helping leaders recognize, decide, or identify what to do next. As I discussed previously, as you become more familiar with the world of the CEO, you will discover just how little is planned ahead for deci-sion making about sources, methods, directions, goals, even aspi-rations. The ability of an advisor to truly fill in the blank spots or provide sensible alternatives is extraordinarily helpful. Most staff people, when with the boss, tend to spend more time whin-ing about other staff functions, the value of various service-type activities, and things that have virtually nothing to do with moving the boss's agenda ahead. Come up with an alternative, a new option, a different way of looking at something in the future, and your influence will grow.

Often, identifying the next step seems terribly mysterious. You may need to search out, assess, evaluate, and recommend additional sources of expertise of value to those who trust you. Additional brains, experience, data, and insight may be required. Be aggressive and forthright in searching out others with answers or with better questions or answers than yours.

Be aware of the assumptions leadership and management hold that create barriers to advice givers:

- We managers and leaders are inherently good communicators. I need other kinds of advice more.
- Operations is always more important than staff functions.
- Some things (such as emergencies) can never really be planned for.
- Things are really better than they seem. We are making prog-ress despite the numbers.
- Outside advice is often more interesting than inside advice.
- Inside advice often seems self-serving or less well informed.

Figure out what you can offer in the way of advice and counsel of a truly strategic nature that may go beyond your staff function, often to a higher level. Ninety-five percent of management decision making involves operational thinking and execution.

Avoid using dollar-equivalent justifications for what you do unless you can clearly and persuasively document a revenue stream into your company or organization, or the actual cost savings as verified by management financial analysis that passes the straight-face test. Management needs proof to believe in the dollar value of staff work. Such justifications have nothing to do with being a trusted strategic advisor, and using a cost-based approach forces management to look at you from a very different perspective. If you set this standard, you will be made to live or die by it.

Focus on outcomes. Focus on tomorrow. Management strategy, management leadership, management problem solving are always about tomorrow, even if the topic is yesterday's mistakes.

Make contributions and suggestions that are self-evidently valuable. Here again, if your proposition costs more but adds little extra value, or if your suggestion might disrupt the organizational structure without bringing a significant increment of improvement, management is very likely to reject what you suggest. Another reason for rejection of advisors' ideas is that they tend to promise more than management believes can be delivered. One important secret: offer fewer suggestions, but make sure that those you do provide have far greater value than their cost.

Say Things That Matter

The trusted strategic advisor, among all the advice givers in the presence of leadership, has the absolute obligation to make certain that whatever he or she offers is truly of value.

Years ago, a former colleague and I, we'll call her Mary Ann, were visiting a client involved in very serious litigation. Mary Ann is quite accomplished and has very special expertise on a

Top Eleven Things You Need to Know to Work Successfully with the Boss

1. Prepare work product in final form. It should be your best, most complete effort.

2. Look at situations from a perspective other than the one the boss has—this leads to interesting, productive discussions that ultimately benefit the client with new ideas and approaches.

3. Think, write, and speak in numbers, bullets, and series.

4. Bring your stories, experiences, and personal history to work—often they reflect an approach or strategy you're trying to explain to a client.

5. Recognize, acknowledge, and learn from the mistakes, missteps, gaffes, and goofs you make—then move on.

6. Be solution driven.

7. Be prepared to explain—succinctly and convincingly—your suggestions, proposals, and recommendations. Speak like someone you'd like to listen to.

8. Remain one step ahead and fifteen minutes early.

9. Anticipate issues, problems, concerns, and opportunities; prepare the boss before he or the client asks; have a plan.

10. Recognize that not every event is a crisis; respond as if every event were a crisis.

11. Speaking for the sake of speaking is unmemorable—*say important things.*

variety of highly technical areas, one of which is Food and Drug Administration regulation. At the end of a very long day of meetings, client confrontations, and hard work, we were walking to our rental car. Mary Ann asked me, "Did I make sense much during the day today, or was I just babbling?"

I responded that we always enjoyed her babbling because it was interesting, informed, and often quite insightful. Then I asked if she noticed what the really highly respected participants did. They tended to ask good questions early in the discussion, and at the end of most discussions they would present ideas, thoughts, and suggestions. The reason for this, I told her quite truthfully, was that there was an expectation by those present that whenever these senior people or outside consultants opened their mouths in meetings, whatever was said had to be profound, powerful, and essential to everyone. It had to be important. Mary Ann might consider, I suggested, waiting until a bit later in the conversation to begin speaking, and making certain that what she said was more functional than conversational. "Say things that matter," I told her.

Mary Ann moved on after a few years, and as I do with every employee who leaves, I asked her to provide her successor with some tips about how best to work with me—or any boss. Her letter contained a fascinating list of eleven items, which I include here as a sidebar. In fact, I remember when she learned each of the lessons in her note. As you'll see, the lesson I describe in the preceding paragraph is number 11 on the list.

Questions to Consider

Here are questions you need to ask yourself about whether you can really put yourself in the boss's shoes and work from a management perspective:

- What is the real expertise, beyond my area of staff knowledge, that I bring to those who run my organization?
- Do I have the patience to make progress incrementally and, at the same time, help the extraordinary number of individuals around me and those who will cross my path as I move toward my goal of becoming a strategic advisor?
- Do I have the stomach for the intense, conflict-ridden, and often confrontational environment in which decisions are made at the senior levels of organizations?
- Do I have the personal patience and substantive intensity to be able to comfortably hold my own among others who do well in these very competitive environments?

- Can I dispassionately assess the strengths, weaknesses, opportunities, options, and threats of the organization from a variety of useful perspectives?

- Do I have access to those who actually have the operating responsibility to resolve issues; implement solutions; and prevent, detect, or deter unproductive actions?

- What am I providing now that is of real value when the boss makes time to speak with me? What can my boss count on from me if I am called in ahead of everyone else?

- What is the benefit to my boss when I am called in ahead of everyone else?

7

THINK STRATEGICALLY

Chapter Outline

Every staff function seems concerned about being more strategic. The words *strategy* and *strategic* are among the most overused by staff people and management. Because my background is in communications, quite early in my career I became tired of hearing these words, only to find that they are used in every other staff function, too. In human resources, the legal department, security, finance, IT, even facilities management, "being a strategic player" and similar notions saturate the staff environment. Despite this overuse, there still appears to be little evidence that staff people truly understand what it means to be strategic or that they are able to recognize what a strategy is.

This chapter holds some surprising insights for you, and will help you have a more productive understanding of the mysterious qualities of strategy and being strategic.

I was once asked to speak at the inaugural meeting of a special trade association consisting solely of the chief litigation officers for America's largest companies. I was somewhat puzzled when I received the request. When I spoke to the gentleman who was contacting me, he said, "We'd like to hear your presentation on developing a strategic mind-set." My response was, "I'm not an attorney. I work with lots of attorneys, but attorneys seem to have a fair amount of juice on their own. Your members must represent literally hundreds of trillions of dollars to their employers." He agreed. So I asked, "They have problems getting to the table anyway?"

His response did astound me: "Even having these very significant dollar responsibilities, attorneys feel that they have difficulty with, and little status in, the strategic decision-making process. Attorneys feel that their clients don't listen to or simply ignore their advice." Here comes the shocker: "We need to be at the table much more frequently, preferably all the time, but especially as strategy is formulated and debated." I had thought that attorneys were always successful in getting themselves welded to the hips of most senior executives.

Well, imagine that: attorneys feeling that they have trouble getting to the table. The rest of us tend to feel that only the attorneys get heard. After my talk, the questions from these high-powered corporate lawyers were direct, and often as naive as those I hear from any other staff function.

The Strategic Perspective

This "lack of hearing" by those in operations causes a tension between staff functions and operating activities that can get in the way of building relationships. Prepare to overcome this tension by focusing on how to address issues more strategically.

Developing a strategic mind-set is crucial to having the relationship, influence, and access that most staff people crave or feel entitled to. We begin the process of thinking about developing a strategic mind-set by understanding what strategy is. I have a rather unusual approach.

You have achieved a strategic mind-set when you are able to verbally inject mental energy into an organization's operational and strategic processes to help leaders and their organizations achieve management objectives.

Strategy is the most crucial product of leadership. It is the ability to be strategic that defines the value of a leader. The reality, as we have seen, is that the higher one goes in an organization, the less actual hands-on work leaders have or need to do. The leader's attention becomes divided among teaching and leading people in the right direction; observing, correcting, and tweaking what is actually going on; and, much of the time, looking over the horizon to identify future destinations, the directions for getting to the future, and the people necessary to make it happen.

Becoming a strategist means committing to a mental approach that out-thinks the competition, the opposition, or the critics and produces a distinctive or unique approach, series of steps, solution options, or choices of direction.

Strategic energy is what drives businesses and organizations, guides leadership, and sets the directions for teams, players, employees, customers, and others. Strategy is the attractant that draws people together and helps them focus on moving in the same direction. Strategy is among the most positive and energizing states of mind. Most of us gravitate toward strategists and leaders for this very reason: they know where we're going, even if they have very little information on the specifics or the mechanics of actually getting there. We want and need to know where we are going.

Strategy focuses the energy and momentum on getting to tomorrow. Assuming that the current plan is based on fundamentally sound information, the advisor's question to himself or herself is, "What part of the overall strategy is my part of the plan helping to accomplish, enhance, or advance?" Are you working on tomorrow or some other destination?

Strategy Is Always Positive

Strategy is always positive and future focused. To strategize about the past is a contradiction. Looking backward is usually negative, and is done only within strict, useful guidelines such as those used for recognizing patterns, as described in Chapter Eight. The strategic thinker is a positive force. This positive focus is what we expect or at least hope for from leaders.

Behaviors that keep us focused on the past are clearly nonstrategic—for example, debating the past, focusing on the unimportant, labeling actions and ideas as strategic (whether they actually are or not), being negative ("Can't do that," "I don't like it," and so on), and making excuses. Teaching the value of staff functions and similar behaviors drain influence and organizational energy and block forward momentum. The wise advisor carefully avoids them. Debating the past is about the most frustrating activity leaders experience. It is such a waste of time.

The Virtues of a Strategist

To begin assessing your strategic capacity, you'll need to ask yourself critical questions about how you approach ideas, questions, opportunities, dangers, and challenges. This portion of the book will help you develop your own list of questions. Use these questions as tools to develop your personal behaviors. Systematically questioning yourself leads to a better understanding of why you choose to be strategic—in other words, what your intentions are for thinking and acting strategically. The result, if you organize it, tends to fall into specific behavior or intention categories I refer to as the virtues of the strategist. Virtues are principles and guidelines for your thinking, behavior, and recommendations. Sometimes they are also expressions of your intentions.

Another benefit of this personal questioning process is that it will help you determine just how strategic you really are or can be. To help accomplish this task, assess yourself against each of the following strategic thinking guidelines or virtues.

Inconsistency

The strategist is intentionally inconsistent. In strategy, inconsistency is a virtue. Strategists relentlessly question all assumptions. The goal, always, is to identify a different approach, to discover new options, to try new and unconventional combinations of ideas and concepts.

Are you predictable? Do you approach most problems in the very same way? Is what you recommend and think about virtually the same in every situation? Are you bound up every time, looking at everything through the lens of your staff function?

Be intentionally different. Grab the wrong end of the telescope. Think about things from a different perspective, intentionally, relentlessly. This is a state of mind.

Advisors of the highest value to leaders and managers are often those who can see things from an entirely different perspective. When you study classic military strategists—Sun Tzu, Von Clausewitz, B. H. Liddell Hart, and others—all stress that one key to victory is acting differently than the opposition expects.

Here is a story where three unexpected actions led to a faster, better, and more humane result. A client of mine operating an educational facility for children with special needs was in a situation where a teacher mistakenly loaned a student a videotape of sexually explicit material, which was subsequently shown to the student's family. The child's father was so irate that he rushed to the school, beat up the teacher, hired a lawyer, and threatened to sue, all in the first three hours of the incident. The facility's standard procedure for responding to allegations was to sit tight, let a little time pass, and see if cooler heads could prevail or if a simple solution might emerge.

My approach was to move much more aggressively. The allegations from this incident were potentially very explosive. Having worked through similar situations in the past, I had learned one big lesson: bad situations like this one ripen badly. Highly emotional situations such as this one, unless dealt with positively and fast, trigger anger, irritation, suspicion, and emotion, which then grow and feed on each other.

Because the head of the school was a man about the same age as the father and both had boys the same age, I suggested that the president immediately write a letter of sympathy, explanation, and apology to this father and offer to meet promptly to work out whatever problems might have been caused by the event. After a brief conversation with the school's attorneys, it was agreed that the letter should be sent directly to the victim's father.

As expected, the father's attorney called, boiling mad, and demanded to know whose idea it was to send this letter. He threatened to file an ethics violation with the local bar association against legal counsel. However, I knew that because the president of the school was not a lawyer, the father of the boy was not an attorney, and I was not an attorney, we were not subject to the rules of legal procedure. Had we followed legal procedure, it might have taken days, weeks, or even longer to schedule a meeting to talk about the situation. As it turned out, this very prompt action on the day of the event triggered a series of meetings that began within seventy-two hours, and a settlement occurred within five working days. Because of its speed and effectiveness, this rapid approach has now become standard operating procedure for this organization. The cost savings in legal fees are enormous, the settlements are achieved quickly and fairly, and, generally, those affected remain clients and customers.

Real Expertise

Technically, your staff function defines the expertise you bring to the table. Being strategic means using your staff experience as a platform to learn even more about the operating areas of the business. You do this for two reasons. First, as I've mentioned elsewhere, most operating executives believe they are sufficiently competent in staff areas and that their need for advice about staff activities is minimal. Second, delving successfully and deeply into an operating area builds your value to management and provides more common ground on which to converse with, advise, and assist operating executives.

A colleague of mine was once approached by a very large refuse hauling company to bid on some consulting work. As he assessed the prospect of doing this, he was warned that this particular company was founded by garbagemen, and tried to hire only other garbagemen. So my colleague went to his local trash hauler and, in exchange for signing a rather complicated and comprehensive release, was allowed to ride on a garbage truck for five days to see what these people do every single day.

As my colleague tells the story, the moment he sat down with his prospective client, he began talking about his experience. He struck a chord with those in the room, and ultimately wound up becoming a long-term outside advisor to this organization. You could argue that he didn't really have substantive expertise, but you also have to admit that very few of us have ever spent even a few minutes, much less five days, riding a garbage truck. The garbage truck–riding strategy was a pretty impressive approach to understanding what the business was really about, especially from the perspective of the business owner or manager. This kind of direct engagement in issues and ideas does impress bosses.

Focus

A strategist applies focus and intensity to the most critical parts of a problem or opportunity using fact finding, truth seeking, and reality testing.

Do you focus primarily on a single aspect of an issue? Do you see problems, issues, and priorities from the boss's perspective? Can you adequately assess and elaborate on the operating benefits of your suggestions and recommendations? Can you hold your own when the conversation turns to operational concerns?

On one occasion, a CEO asked me to sit in and help work through the process of establishing a five- to ten-year, forward-looking picture for the company. They had hired a very experienced facilitator from one of the large consulting companies. He had an excellent reputation.

As the meeting opened, it was clear that there was going to be some difficulty in establishing a time frame in which to hypothesize. After forty-five minutes of struggle to get some traction, I raised my hand, and I asked the CEO how long he had been in office. He replied, "About twenty months." I then asked how long his predecessor had served as CEO. He said, "About thirty-seven months." I then asked about the predecessor before that, and his answer was, "About forty-two months." I then turned to the facilitator and the group and suggested, "Why don't we begin by hypothesizing the next eighteen to twenty months, the likely length of time the current CEO will be in office, and see where that will take us." There was an audible gasp in the group, followed by a short period of silence. I'm sure they were all thinking that my service as a consultant had just ended. However, the meeting got on track almost immediately, and they were able to move forward and come up with a more satisfactory set of ideas and concepts. I did get to go home early.

The question you're constantly asking so as to achieve and maintain substantive intensity is, "Does what we're doing now really matter?" If not, move on, or end the meeting.

It's what gets done that matters. The strategist focuses on what the business needs to get done, in priority order. The strategist consistently asks, "What is the singular importance of what I'm doing? What is its relevance to achieving management's most crucial objectives?"

Constantly gravitating toward the most important actions, decisions, behaviors, and outcomes is a key ingredient in being an effective strategist.

Laggership and Entropy

A strategist understands the power of setting priorities. The strategist also understands the power of timing responses or the initiation of additional action, at least for a brief period of time. Choosing to wait, to hold back, is always a very serious strategy decision. Strategy is basically about exploring a full range of options, from doing nothing to taking aggressive action.

Laggership   To engage in laggership is to act promptly, but not necessarily immediately. It's waiting, watching, or standing by, just momentarily.

The analogy for laggership is the military patrol, exploring enemy territory. The shortest life expectancy is that of the person at the point of the patrol who will have first contact. My preference is to be in the third or fourth rank so that I have the opportunity to see where the bullets are coming from and have a better chance of surviving to return and report to headquarters.

Entropy   Entropy is a term from physics that describes the tendency of virtually all systems and activities to degrade, decline, and disintegrate if there is no addition of energy and resources. Fail to service your car regularly, and it will become unsafe and eventually fall apart. Fail to nurture and maintain relationships, and they too degrade and eventually come apart. Using entropy as a strategy is to choose to let things happen or to "do nothing" and see what will develop.

———————

These two concepts are related and are quite strategic in their application to management decision making. Most staff people have a bias for action. The strategist looks at a range of action options, choosing two or three after study and evaluation, and within the context of these strategic virtues. The advantage of thinking this way is that the strategist now has three different ways to describe a very powerful point in developing a management strategy: laggership, entropy, or simply "doing nothing."

To some extent, I purposely choose memorable language, even words I have invented and therefore need to explain, such as laggership. To an attorney, doing nothing often means just that. Should the suggestion to do nothing come from an attorney, that is undoubtedly what will happen until a substantial reaction is required. If the boss thinks about "doing nothing," it's likely that doing nothing will be the strategic choice until a colleague or peer calls and perhaps chews him or her out for being overly timid. Or the boss's mother calls and asks why something isn't being done. In the latter two scenarios, something is likely to happen or change.

In particularly grave situations, doing nothing can be catastrophically bad; even the appearance of doing nothing can cause serious damage. But the idea of being more prudent and thoughtful clearly falls within the range of strategic decision making.

Pragmatism

A strategist attempts to clarify, refine, and carefully target; to deal in facts, truth, and reality-based information; and, wherever possible, to forecast results that can actually or reasonably be achieved, while also recognizing the unintended consequences of various action options. A pragmatist usually forecasts underwhelming results.

As I mentioned in Chapter Five, another way I define a pragmatist is as an individual who gets the getable, knows the knowable, does the doable, and achieves the achievable.

Pragmatism is often considered the opposite of, or certainly very different from, optimism. As discussed in Chapter One, being overly optimistic and failing to accurately estimate, evaluate, and forecast the outcomes of their activities are two of the most significant reasons leaders lose their positions. Pragmatism is the antidote for excessive optimism. Can you and do you accurately forecast the intended and unintended results of your recommendations?

Incrementalism

Anyone who has run anything for any length of time learns pretty quickly that all progress occurs in increments, and rarely in giant leaps. Proposals and ideas, which suggest that giant leaps are possible, are generally suspect in operational terms.

The strategist recognizes that most everything in the life of an organization gets done one step at a time, and sometimes in only fractions of a step at a time. The issue is absolute progress rather than the quantity or even the quality of the progress. The strategist is driven by the relentless desire and urgency to move ahead, to find the next constructive increment and achieve it, so that we can see what the next increment will be.

Do you manage the expectations of those you advise—that is, to expect fewer but more significant increments? In other words, can you move your own approach closer to the incremental model (small but constant improvement) and away from the silver bullet (one big change all at once)?

Thinking Strategically

Many years ago, I came across an interesting discussion of strategic thinking in a book by the Japanese consultant Kenichi Ohmae, *The Mind of the Strategist: Business Planning for Competitive Advantage* (1991). An illustration, also called "The Mind of a Strategist" (p. 14), held a surprise epiphany for me.

Ohmae's key insight, for me, is his analysis comparing three management thinking methodologies: mechanical systems thinking (I call this linear thinking), intuition, and strategic thinking. Let me talk about each of them as I've come to understand them and teach them to others. The goal here is to help you understand as well, so that you can teach others, too.

Linear Thinkers

The linear thinker, or process thinker if you prefer, is the trained or experienced manager, boss, or specialist; the physician, economist, MBA, engineer, scientist, or typical CEO. Linear thinking is typified by a more structured, process-driven, or step-by-step approach. Linear thinkers are the people who, as Stephen Covey would

Figure 7.1 Management Thinking (Linear or Process Thinking)

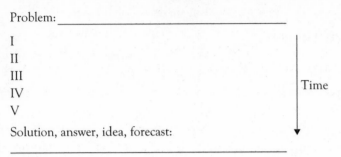

Problem: _____

I

II

III

IV   Time

V

Solution, answer, idea, forecast:

say, plan with the end in mind, using management structure and formats, chronologies, order of manufacture, and so on to get things done.

Almost all senior leaders are largely linear thinkers. Figure 7.1 illustrates the heart of the management thinking process. When confronted with a problem, the manager first divides that problem into its major constituent elements (represented by the roman numerals) and then begins working and reworking those elements over time (represented by the arrow on the right) for the purpose of arriving at a solution, answer, idea, or forecast. When planning, the manager early on identifies the end to be achieved or the problem to be resolved and constructs a process backward from the end to include every detail, up to and through start-up or start-over, to achieve the goal. Whether dealing with a problem or planning for the future, managers and other leaders employ this process approach, predictable but useful for its simplicity, structure, and focus on resolution.

Linear thinkers can easily intimidate creative or intuitive people because linear thinkers seem so organized, so "logical," so . . . well, linear. It is a serious discipline to become and remain a linear thinker—to constructively see the world in process increments. It's part of developing a management mind-set (see Chapter Six).

Management may relate better to the staff functions that use similar thinking and intellectual strategies—law, finance, accounting, and IT—than to the more intuitive approaches of communications, human resources, or strategic planning.

Intuitive Thinkers

The intuitive thinker is a person whose mind is extraordinarily different from that of the process thinker. The intuitive mind has a significant amount of random experience from life "floating around" that "gets triggered" by having to find immediate or deadline-driven solutions and answers. As you can imagine, the linear and intuitive styles are vastly different ways of thinking that will often conflict. Creative people, such as artists, painters, news reporters, and writers, are mostly intuitive thinkers. Corporate functions requiring high levels of creativity or people focus—human resources, communications, and security—also tend to be highly intuitive.

Intuitive people often actually avoid analytical approaches. Their goal is to find the great idea or the most interesting or creative solution—the silver bullet or a nonlinear solution—because the issues faced are highly emotional or perceptual. Linear thinkers are often frustrated by the extemporaneous, often serendipitous nature of intuitive advice.

If you're an intuitive thinker, chances are you can operate on pretty short deadlines, marshal a lot of information relatively quickly, and be ready to act on short notice. Also, ideas come to you far more rapidly than to the linear or process thinker. In fact, intuitive thinkers' brains are, in a sense, like vast storehouses (I often make the comparison to wastebaskets as a better concept) for dozens, perhaps thousands, of ideas and fragments of thoughts or concepts—just lots of stuff. Any number of these fragments can be activated and articulated through an experience, a word, a photograph, or someone else's presentation.

In Figure 7.2, each dot or circle represents an experience, fragment or factoid, idea or concept simply floating around in the intuitive thinker's mind waiting to be activated, primarily by

Figure 7.2 Intuitive Thinking

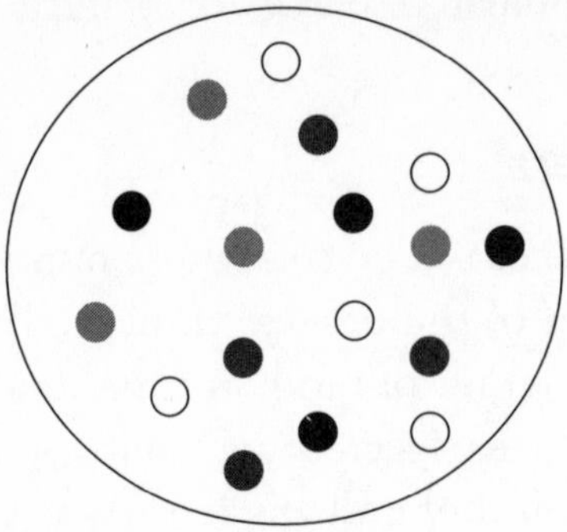

Source: Copyright © 2007, The Lukaszewski Group, Inc. All rights reserved. Reproduction without written permission of the copyright owner is strictly prohibited.

a deadline rather than a process to seek a solution. If process is called for, the intuitive thinker will leapfrog to the end and start working there first. This is another frustration for linear thinkers: "Let's do things in proper order" or "How can you know what the end will look like if you haven't worked on the beginning and the middle yet?"

The Making Jell-O® Phenomenon is a good way to describe how the intuitive thinker works. You have all made Jell-O or at least know what it is. You boil the water, stir in the powder until it is dissolved, put the bowl in the refrigerator, and at some point—we're not exactly sure when (there may be a deal between God and Kraft Foods)—Jell-O happens. It is amazing. It is mysterious. Yet the result is expected.

Where the linear thinker is driven by a timeline, a chronology, and a structured outline with basically all its elements known, the intuitive thinker is simply driven by a deadline—the magic power of Jell-O. The ingredients floating around suddenly come together to produce the desired effect or outcome. There is little long-range thinking about how things will turn out. With the intuitive thinker, it is all very last minute and just before the deadline (when the Jell-O Phenomenon happens). It is unexplainable.

It is a mystery. With the intuitive thinker, if there is no deadline, there is no progress or solution.

It is this spontaneous, seeming shallowness and lack of evidence that makes the linear thinker uncomfortable with intuition-driven approaches. This discomfort (and distrust) frustrates the intuitive thinker because "they [linear thinkers] always require proof that an idea or suggestion will work."

For advice generated by intuitive thinking to be recognized, understood, and taken seriously, it must be translated into a process methodology that managers can more readily absorb and act on. Intuitive thinkers can translate their ideas and concepts into the process methodology in three ways, through the creation of checklists, prioritized lists, or sequences of events. The Three-Minute Drill in Chapter Nine is an extremely useful translation tool.

Strategic Thinkers

The strategic thinker takes intentionally different approaches—every time. All assumptions are suspended or questioned. As I discussed earlier, inconsistency is a key virtue of strategic thinking. The strategist consciously, relentlessly, and purposely seeks different approaches. The strategist is intentionally going for an unusual, unexpected result. Paraphrasing Ohmae's interpretation, strategic thinking is a process involving four phases: problem identification; analysis and weighing of constituents; deconstruction and scenario development based on different configurations of constituents or options; and creative reintegration.

One of my favorite stories about strategic thinking comes from Dr. Edward DeBono. As he describes the situation in Great Britain early in World War II, when the Battle of Britain was going on and the Germans were inflicting enormous losses on British aircraft, British engineers were working constantly to reinforce the airplanes against damage from attack, but their efforts were largely unsuccessful. It was a frustrating and frightening time.

Then, after weeks of constantly studying the aircraft return-ing to Britain that had survived enemy fire, one engineering group had an amazing idea. They realized that the damage sustained by the surviving planes must be on different parts of the aircraft than the damage inflicted on the planes that were not recovered for analysis. Therefore, they thought, rather than reinforce the damaged areas, why not reinforce the areas that were *not* damaged? This dramatic change in thinking had a significant impact on the survivability of aircraft and was one of the ingredients that helped Britain prevail in the air battles leading up to the major actions in World War II.

Another fascinating story involving strategic thinking relates to the discovery of fiber optics. When it was discovered that glass fibers could carry data, the race was on to apply this technology for the purpose of replacing conventional methods, such as cop-per wire. Virtually every major glass company in conjunction with many university laboratories were looking for ways to purify differ-ent types of glass, the theory being that the purest glass could carry the most signal packets with the greatest efficiency.

At DowCorning in New York, through a chance discovery using a fiber material containing several known impurities, it was discovered that impure glass could carry more data than pure glass. So the company's scientists rerouted their efforts from purifying glass fibers to determining what the best impurities would be to add into the manufactured glass to enhance the transmission of data. DowCorning dominates the fiber-optic cable market today.

Examination of Ohmae's diagram (Figure 7.3) shows just how different the three thinking styles are.

Phase I: Identification   The problem is identified, and background knowledge or relevant patterns are applied. In Figure 7.3, the same problem is examined in the context of each thinking style.

- The linear thinker begins applying a symmetrical concepts approach, more to reconfigure than to reinvent.

Figure 7.3 The Mind of the Strategist

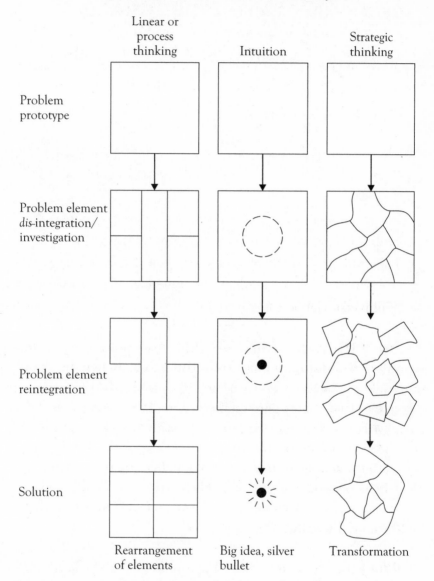

Source: Adapted from *The Mind of a Strategist,* by Kenichi Ohmae © 1991. Reproduced with permission of the McGraw-Hill Companies.

- The intuitive thinker immediately begins to seek a critical fact, idea, notion, or insight among a host of other potential ideas and concepts.

- The strategic thinker is from the start creatively deconstructing the problem in ways that are unique and outside expected patterns. The pattern of assumptions made by the intuitive and linear thinkers is totally subject to challenge in the strategist's mind.

Phase II: Differentiation

- The linear thinker begins looking in a symmetrical way to reconfigure the problem in various, sometimes even innovative, ways.
- The intuitive thinker begins pushing away the extraneous, continuing to seek a significantly different idea or approach.
- The strategic thinker continues purposely deconstructing the problem in ways that are different, unusual, and in search of a surprising result.

Phase III: Deconstruction   All three thinking styles are beginning to fashion their solutions and are at the extreme edge of their approach to deconstructing the problem. This phase is where the significantly different approach of the strategist begins to show. This is also the phase that makes both the linear thinker and the intuitive thinker a little nervous. Thinking that goes too "far out" in the corporate and institutional environments is often cause for concern and is considered very risky.

Phase IV: Creative Reintegration

- During this phase, the linear thinker has produced a fairly symmetrical concept that may actually be quite innovative but is also expected or predictable.
- The intuitive thinker has found the silver bullet, the big idea, and will take it to management as the magic solution for a problem.

- The strategic thinker has developed a decidedly nonlinear, complex, unexpected, even strange response. This is what strategic thinkers do. They are inconsistent; they are different; they think from different altitudes and attitudes with the goal of coming up with something unique and, they hope, important, powerful, and conclusive.

As you compare these approaches in Figure 7.3, you see a graphic illustration of the differences in the product these thinking styles produce.

The *linear thinker's solution* is symmetrical. It adds up, has balance, and to a certain degree resembles the original problem. This comment can be confusing. The example I often use involves big organizations coming out of bankruptcy or other powerful business situations, where the changes they ultimately make after much study, investment, and gnashing of teeth seem relatively minor. An airline comes out of bankruptcy, and the first thing it does is to repaint the aircraft and change the company stationery. Another example is the large retailer, following a huge reorganization, that takes as its first initiative the changing of the uniforms of those who work with customers. You could characterize these solutions as lacking boldness. They resemble the original problems.

The *intuitive thinker's solution* is the classic silver bullet. This is the response, idea, or action that will solve the problem in one amazing, perhaps single, action or activity. Magic solutions are extraordinarily rare. Few examples really come to mind: penicillin, an accidental discovery; the transistor, the result of a brainstorm of scientists at Bell Laboratories; the lightbulb, a simple device invented by Thomas Edison after five thousand unsuccessful attempts; the I-beam architecture used in buildings that led to structures so high that elevators were invented to replace staircases; the World Wide Web. Although dramatic and interesting, these life- and society-changing concepts are very, very few indeed.

The *strategist's solution,* though utilizing elements of the original problem, produces a distinct and unique solution that often looks very little like the original problem. A strategist's goal is to transform the problem prototype into a command opportunity, a command strategy, a series of actions leading to a powerful result or series of results. Clearly, strategic thinking is the most challenging of the three. The goals are different, and its approaches are different. In many respects, the product of strategic thinking can make management action very unconventional, but also very powerful. Good examples of counterintuitive thinking include Teflon, 3M Post-it notes, microwave ovens, corneal transplants, and heart pacemakers.

In real life, good managers and decision makers, even staff people, are situational thinkers. They must also be intuitive and strategic. They remain always process sensitive. The key to integrating the various types of thinking into a process for implementing strategy is to translate the results of that thinking into language and action plans that those affected can understand, support, and execute.

It is essential that advisors who are intuitive thinkers explain how their thinking process works to those they advise. I use the diagrams in this chapter and the discussion to help those I counsel understand why I think the way I do, the kinds of solution options to expect, and that my intention is to come at their problems from different points of view. After all, if all you do in a room is repeat ideas and concepts that others can provide, perhaps with more credibility than you have, what are you doing there?

Why Some Strategies Are Flawed from the Start

Many proposed strategies—seemingly brilliant though they may be in the eyes of staff advisors—stay glued to the drawing board. Some strategies can't be executed for lots of pretty simple reasons: they're unworkable, unethical, sometimes irresponsible; they may be lacking in power. In my experience, the following are the five most common fatal flaws in strategy:

1. **Not really part of a strategic interest.** A strategy may be foolproof, but if its objective doesn't align with the larger corporate strategy, it is beside the point.

2. **Can't be supported by management.** Some solutions or strategies may be too complicated—may cut across too many internal political and operational barriers, create substantial unintended future consequences, or simply seem too risky.

3. **Developed without input from the boss.** This is probably the most common reason for strategies to fail. Staff people mistakenly work through elaborate processes and procedures, getting everything "ready to go," and then present their findings or approaches to the boss, who is, of course, totally stunned by what has gone on, especially as there was no input from the boss in the first place.

4. **Usurps the legitimate territory of others.** This might be better stated, "Gives the appearance of infringing on the territory of others as recognized by the others." The complaint that some course of action originated in the wrong place within the organization is quite often difficult to overcome or is even insurmountable.

5. **Avoids dealing with truly tough stuff.** Where are those advisors who knew better when hundreds of American CEOs thought that backdating stock options was "probably legal"? They are gone, but so are the CEOs, general counsels, and CFOs. When staff keep quiet to protect their jobs, rather than ruffle feathers by offering the strategies, options, and warnings bosses need to survive truly critical situations, career-defining moments for bosses often occur.

Becoming and being a strategic player is a difficult and challenging discipline to master. Most management environments

treat those who are inconsistent and challenging as argumenta-
tive and obstructive. At first, you'll learn to put your strategic hat
on only when those things that really matter are at stake. Having some success with this approach will embolden you to adopt
more broadly strategic behaviors and attitudes. Management will
need to test before they trust, verify before they trust, authenticate
before they trust. Keep the positive pressure on, and the value of
your strategic efforts will powerfully speak for itself.

Can You Develop a Strategic Mind-Set?

As I noted at the outset of the chapter, the words *strategy* and *strategic* are the two most overused words in the lexicon of business and
leadership. Staff people like to use them but rarely can define them
in terms of management decision making. When I work with the
various staff functions, one of the first questions I'm asked when
the boss is not around is, "What is strategy, exactly?" The second
question is, "How can I act more strategically?" That's because when
you work with leaders, it becomes pretty clear that they are strategists and that to be in their presence and offer advice successfully you
need to have this capacity as well. These questions are designed to
help you determine just how strategic you already are, and the work
you have yet to do to become a strategist. Ask yourself:

- Can I develop a flexible approach to problems? (Or do I
  approach most problems in the very same way every time?)
  Can I truly be inconsistent—that is, look for different
  approaches constantly?

- Have I developed an understanding of the business that goes
  sufficiently beyond my staff function to enable a strategic
  approach?

- Have I explained to those I counsel how I think and analyze
  problems, questions, and issues, so that they will relate to
  what I will recommend about the boss's problems, issues, and
  priorities?

- Do I understand how my actions and advice are relevant to achieving management's most crucial objectives?
- Am I constantly asking myself, *Does this really matter?* or *What matters more?*
- Do I have a bias for action while still questioning all decision assumptions?
- Do I focus on what is doable rather than the ideal?
- Can I candidly explore the limitations of my own thinking and ideas, and share those limitations with those I advise?

If you can answer yes to most of these questions, you are well on the way to developing a truly strategic mind-set.

8

BE A WINDOW TO TOMORROW

Understand the Power of Patterns

Chapter Outline

Study the Patterns That Past Scenarios Yield

The Strategic Value of Pattern-Related Thinking

Pattern Examples

    Corporate succession

    Corporate restructuring

    Mergers and acquisitions

    The plant shutdown

Exposure Management and Surveillance

    Phase I: Identify corporate exposure sources, issues, and threats

    Phase II: Compute response priorities

    Phase III: Issue confidential exposure reports

    Phase IV: Meet quarterly for exposure review

War Stories

The Lessons of Pattern and Scenario Awareness

Lesson 1: Patterns are the foundation of strategy and are what make the strategist an intelligent forecaster

Lesson 2: War story files are one tool advisors can use to help the boss better understand a situation and all its ramifications as a pattern of events unfolds

Lesson 3: Preemptively translate relevant patterns and problems into useful strategic tools management can use before problems occur

Lesson 4: Focus most of your work on nonoperating scenarios

Lesson 5: Talking about patterns is often a powerful way to be memorable

Can You Recognize What's Coming Next?

The chief executive of a large regional bank headquartered in the southeastern United States invited me to work with his chief operating officer to improve the COO's board presentation skills and to prepare him for some extensive public visibility with respect to a new regional corporate initiative. Little did I anticipate the fireworks that would begin shortly after I arrived.

Our initial meeting was scheduled to take place in the Corporate Training Center, which had the appropriate technology and support facilities. I arrived early; the COO, who was almost always early, wasn't there. I called his office to check with his administrative assistant, who told me that as far as she knew he had planned to be there. After an hour, there was still no COO.

Ninety minutes into our scheduled time, he arrived. He was obviously upset, irritated, and about to explode. His first comment, I recall, was, "I'm going to kill the S.O.B." My response was, "And which S.O.B. would that be?" His response was, "There's only one," and he named, of course, the chairman. Clearly, the agenda for the day had just evaporated, so I asked him to grab a cup of coffee, sit down, and talk it through. As it turns out, he'd had breakfast that morning with the chairman, who casually informed him that he was contemplating putting the bank up for sale. This infuriated the COO, of course, because up until breakfast time, he'd assumed, on the basis of positive indications from the chairman, that he was going to be the new chief executive upon the boss's retirement. All that was about to change; twenty years of work, dedication, and anticipation were about to be flushed down the drain.

Incidentally, during my briefing by the chairman about what he expected from the work I was to do with the COO, the chairman told me that he was planning to retire within twenty-four months and that unless something happened during that time frame, the COO would be his successor. That was extremely confidential. I kept that to myself.

The COO and I spent the next two hours walking through the inevitable and incredible pattern that virtually all succession strategies follow, beginning, of course, with a review of the three main stages of leadership of an organization: finding the bathroom, getting something done, and establishing one's legacy or immortality. Clearly the chairman was moving seriously into the immortality phase.

There's nothing like a succession scenario to trigger the yearning in the chief executive to be remembered permanently in the future and to make every effort to ensure that his or her pet projects, ideas, and concepts cannot be changed by some future CEO, even if that individual is of the CEO's own choosing. Every time CEOs plan to leave an organization, their thoughts turn to legacy and immortality.

The COO and I talked about likely scenarios, the first, of course, being that the longer the chairman stays in office, contemplating succession, the less likely it is that his first choice, this COO, will survive the gauntlet the chairman would no doubt set up during the next twenty-four months. Once CEOs go into succession mode, they undergo a definite behavior shift: they begin to torpedo their putative successors. In fact, anytime a retirement is announced more than ten or twelve months into the future, the likely successor at the time of the announcement becomes less and less likely to be the successor when retirement ultimately occurs. What gets executed is the successor's career. Count on this as part of the pattern.

The COO and I talked about many things that day, but the most important were these: becoming the successor was up to the successor to accomplish rather than the CEO. "Starting today, suck it up, deal with it, keep your temper in check, and focus on getting through what's about to happen," I said. I told him to expect the CEO to invent lots of new ideas, to micromanage and intervene. The closer retirement gets, the more many CEOs feel that the place still needs them to survive. I told the COO that because in this case the CEO had decided he wanted to try to sell the bank, the COO's job, first and foremost, was to step forward, volunteer to chair the selling effort, and carry it out with the highest possible level of effectiveness.

We also talked about the fact that whatever the chairman has done can be undone the moment the successor takes office. "Stop worrying about what's not getting done," I told him. "Many of the things you'd like to do to prepare for succession will be blocked, and you will be prohibited from doing anything substantive until you have those three magic letters, CEO, by your name. It's true, selling the company can change all that, but the odds of selling this bank, at this time, in this market, involves a great deal of optimism."

"But he's not making any efforts or steps to plan for a transition period," the COO complained. My response was, "Well, duh. If he gets hit by a bus tomorrow, you can step in. If you can survive for twenty-four months, he'll allow you to succeed him, and you can step in then. Ideal transition and succession scenarios are often things only management theorists from business schools tend to write about."

After we met for about five and a half hours, the COO went back to his office to organize his thoughts with a whole new perspective on how to survive the next twenty-four months. I walked over to see the chairman and to tell him three things:

1. This was the last assignment that I could do for him, because he had selected new leadership, and my attention now had to shift to the COO's best interests.

2. That the CEO should grab his wife of thirty-seven years, Thelma; rent a Winnebago next week; take a corporate check-book along; visit every one of their 340 branches through-out the Southeast; write checks; get in the newspaper; have community dinners and celebrations of this institution's work in the community, his personal work, and this vision of his impending retirement. This would allow the COO to learn to run the place in his absence.

3. Surprise everyone by retiring at least nine to ten months ahead of his announced schedule.

With that, I left and went back to New York. That was that. Actually, that was the only time I spent with the COO and the last time I spent any time with the CEO.

Seven years, almost to the day, after that meeting, I got a phone call from the COO, who introduced himself as the CEO of the bank. He asked if I remembered him, and I said I certainly did. He said that he was beginning to contemplate his own retirement, and he recalled that he and I had met for a single day. He didn't remember precisely what had happened during that day, but he wondered if I was still helping in succession situations. Would I mind if his intended successor called me to get some advice? I responded that I remembered the day minute by minute and that if he'd like to review it, I'd be happy to refresh his memory. Perhaps he'd like to have me do it with his successor on the line. Or, of course, his successor could give me a call. And by the way, I asked him, what was his intended retirement date? He laughed and said, "Well, it's coming up pretty quickly—about six to eight months."

His successor never did call, but I know for a fact that the transition went off without a hitch.

Study the Patterns That Past Scenarios Yield

One of the great insights I gained very early in my career (in fact I have long forgotten where it happened) was about the power of patterns. It is often said that those who fail to study and learn from history are doomed to repeat it. My experience is the opposite. No matter how much we study history, we will undoubtedly repeat significant portions of it. The objective of pattern analysis is to pay strategic attention to what the key elements, timelines, and repetitive events reveal, and use those insights to anticipate the future.

Learning the repetitive patterns of decisions, behaviors, and mistakes that key historical events illustrate, often in the same order, is the incentive to study these events as potential future scenarios. Such study and analysis yield significant insight into likely event sequences, actions, or decision schedules, and can expose the range of outcomes and the options available to change outcomes.

Often when I talk about this, especially in connection with the scenario planning required to be appropriately prepared for many serious management situations, the push-back I'll get is that a particular client's market, culture, product line, or history is unique, and that therefore what's happened before can't possibly be relevant to what's going to happen. Experience teaches the opposite. But we still hear the old bromide that a "cookie-cutter approach" will fail. What you learn as a strategic advisor is that quite often a cookie cutter will help stabilize the situation and begin to counteract the new patterns so that there is far less damage from collateral consequences caused by genuinely new or unique aspects of the situation. The reality of what patterns teach is that cookie cutters actually work—again and again and again—precisely because history does repeat itself. Cookie cutters actually allow for faster response to urgent situations and provide immediate, experientially based action options. A patterned approach beats guessing and the communal decision making so evident when management is faced with unfamiliar, explosive, or toxic circumstances.

In Chapter Seven, I talked about inconsistency as a virtue of strategy. Now that we are studying the value of patterns, it seems that there is a contradiction here. But, in fact, one of the brain-busting attributes of strategists is that they can deal with this kind of ambiguity and resist the urge to set absolute pathways for making important decisions. The strategist relies on a variety of tools and disciplines. Among the most important is a healthy skepticism about the past. Patterns are helpful because they lead to the future, but they are also risky because they allow us to make assumptions based on the past that may or may not be helpful or even true. Rather than be confused, accept the fact that pattern expertise is an essential discipline.

The Strategic Value of Pattern-Related Thinking

If you understand patterns, then you systematically discipline yourself to observe events and scenarios with an eye for analyzing event structure, timelines, and variables. Two powerful benefits accrue to you. First, you simply know more than other people because most people think in fragments, in segments, often in a state of denial. This approach can create even more devastating problems. Second, you can become a forecaster. This is the powerful part. Although there is some truth to the observation that scenarios or patterns have their unique characteristics, what is even more powerfully true is that they also share enormously important, often crucial similarities. This being the case, you can make forecasts about strategies, approaches, and outcomes. The magic of this insight is that although you'll be wrong at least 50 percent of the time, you'll be right almost half the time. You'll be considered a bloomin' genius.

Pattern Examples

From both management and communications perspectives, patterns provide powerful indications that if ignored or carelessly addressed can cause even the most crucial strategic intentions to come apart, fail, or bring about even more problems. Even the most adverse of circumstances and the worst of surprises have recognizable elements and reasonably similar event sequences. Here are some examples.

Corporate Succession

The story with which I opened this chapter illustrates a typical corporate succession pattern. The shorter the period of time between the publicly announced end of one leader's tenure to the succession of the next, the more likely it is that what is planned will actually occur. This is the pattern of success. In the pattern of failure, the current chair announces his or her intention to retire twenty-four to thirty months out, names a successor, then spends the remainder of the term of office trying to establish his or her immortality, build his or her legacy, and torpedo whatever it is the incoming successor might plan to accomplish.

Corporate Restructuring

Often announced with big ballyhoo, projections of substantial cost savings, and perhaps even some new directions, restructurings are frequently accompanied by substantial cuts in employment combined with justifications and reorganizations. What is less often reported is that the proposed savings are more than consumed by the incredible cost of laying off hundreds, perhaps thousands, of individuals. The turmoil caused by restructuring is often so destructive that it leads key people essential to the success of the fundamental concept to leave. The cycle repeats itself, usually within a few months or years.

Mergers and Acquisitions

Virtually all mergers and acquisitions are takeovers in one respect or another. If you've worked for the company with less than 51 percent equity, even though the merger or acquisition was described as "the perfect combination of two great companies," you know firsthand that it was really a takeover. The acquired company goes through a pattern of paralysis, loss of momentum, and loss of key people while everyone waits for the plan to be announced and implemented. Ironically, similar patterns are occurring in the acquiring company.

Although there is eagerness to get on with the job and absorb the acquired institution, room has to be made, at least temporarily, for some key executives and officers from the acquired firm. Even though everyone's life is in total chaos, this is supposed to send a positive signal that keeps folks working and producing.

Lots of paper may have changed hands, but the deal usually takes longer than planned to finalize and looks quite different from whatever was originally envisioned. By the time things are ultimately squared away, the really valuable people in the acquired firm are beginning to execute their departure strategies, while many others are simply cut.

With regard to due diligence, there is often such pressure put on by the CEOs of the two major players to do the deal that rigorous analysis is actually avoided. Betting the entire business is one of the most exciting games top executives ever get to play. Once takeovers are set in motion, only extraordinary events (internal or external) or a marketplace or governmental intervention can stop these deals from going forward. This is another crucial reason why nearly all acquisitions and mergers fail in most respects. Even so, there are those who always benefit and become extremely wealthy as a result.

The Plant Shutdown

In the typical scenario, the decision to close a plant and reduce operations is made "secretly" by a small group of executives and then shared with a larger working group within a day or so. The target date is set for sixty to ninety days in the future (though sometimes it is set for six months to a year ahead) so that "preparations" can be made internally to manage the process and for compliance with various local, state, and federal laws and regulations.

Naturally, as the supposedly secret plan proceeds, word and rumors leak out (sometimes within hours of the original decision). Rumors of the shutdown plans often cause sudden and powerful increases in productivity and quality at the affected facility. The announcement is finally made (it may have been delayed two or three times due to "corporate scheduling"). Everyone in the affected facility is totally puzzled by the decision because they have been performing so well that "certainly someone would have noticed by now." The decision is firm; the plant is scheduled for closing.

The unions announce that they and their international parent are working with a Wall Street investment banker to find a white knight to purchase the facility from the parent company. Failing that, the group will attempt an employee buyout in the hope that they can operate the facility themselves. High work quality and productivity continue, yet the parent company's decision remains firm. No buyers are found. The plant ultimately, belatedly closes.

Exposure Management and Surveillance

As I've noted elsewhere, the filtration of information gets so severe as it nears the top of an organization that most senior executives, and especially the CEO, feel that what they receive is overly strained and refined. One of the trusted strategic advisor's most important roles is to ensure that crucial information makes it to the top very promptly. My term for this process is *exposure management and surveillance*, the purposeful monitoring of key corporate exposure sources and issues. The five goals of exposure management and surveillance are to

1. Alert the top manager to possible threats and opportunities, and the patterns they represent.
2. Anticipate the organization's planned and unplanned visibility, internally and externally.
3. Prepare management to act promptly, conclusively, and pragmatically, once they recognize the scenario.
4. Work preemptively to mitigate and perhaps eliminate potential problems and threats.
5. Estimate the potential organizational impact and exposure from threats, opportunities, and other circumstances.

This information is provided to the CEO in just two pages. These reports are so highly sensitive that distribution is only at the discretion of the CEO. Figure 8.1 illustrates a type of exposure management and surveillance program structure.

Figure 8.1 Exposure Management and Surveillance Process

Phase I
Identify Corporate Exposure Sources, Issues, and Threats

A. Identify Actions, Decisions, Events, and Activities to Monitor
Select those with special significance for impact and threat analysis in part B.

B. Forecast Impact and Threat Levels
1. Score each of these items on a scale of 1 to 10, where 10 equals the highest level of impact.
2. Score each of these items on a scale of 1 to 10, where 10 equals the highest degree of threat.

___ Activist demonstrations/threats
___ Angry neighbors
___ Competitive breakthroughs
___ Congressional testimony
___ Corporate liability
___ Criminal investigations
___ Employee unrest
___ Executive speeches
___ Government investigations
___ Hazardous waste
___ High-profile litigation
___ International sanctions
___ Key executive public appearances
___ Labor negotiations or actions
___ Major site-specific issues
___ Risk management plan (RMP)
___ Serious environmental cases
___ Significant news interviews
___ Superfund
___ Whistle-blowers

___/___ Adverse court decisions
___/___ Angry employees
___/___ Anti-corporate action
___/___ Congressional hearings
___/___ Emergency potential
___/___ Emerging issue or problem
___/___ Exquisite threat
___/___ Indictment of managers or employees
___/___ Internal documents leaked
___/___ Major management decisions
___/___ Major media story
___/___ Plant closing
___/___ Product problems
___/___ Prosecution
___/___ Protestors
___/___ Regulatory problems
___/___ Takeovers
___/___ Whistle-blowers
___/___ _____

Phase II
Compute Response Priorities

Add the impact and threat numbers from phase I together to arrive at a combined score. List up to five items with the highest scores here, in descending order. These are your highest-priority issues for exposure management, surveillance, and readiness activity.

1. _____   4. _____

2. _____   5. _____

3. _____

Phase III
Issue Confidential Exposure Reports

Write a synopsis for each of the issues or threats listed in phase II. Each synopsis should explore why the issue or threat is of utmost importance to the organization, the specific impact to be expected, and the consequences of failing to be ready.

• Number all copies • Prohibit any duplication or faxing • Collect copies after 72 hours • Revise surveillance and exposure goals and adjust readiness plans to reflect new information and current situation

Phase IV
Meet Quarterly for Exposure Review

• Identify new vulnerabilities • Eliminate old vulnerabilities • Provide feedback for revisions to response plan

Phase I: Identify Corporate Exposure Sources, Issues, and Threats

Part A lists major categories of threats and circumstances, ranging from labor negotiations to site-specific issues, even executive speeches and key public appearances. For each of these elements, the list is customized to fit the organization, and each element is scored to reflect its level of exposure threat to the organization. In part B, the specific areas of threat are scored for their impact on the organization, should they occur. To complete phase I, the scores of each item are tabulated, and the three with the highest score are then placed in the Compute Response Priorities box for phase II.

Phase II: Compute Response Priorities

The purpose of this section is to highlight the highest-scoring threat circumstances from phase I and to prioritize them even further to determine where the highest level of management attention needs to be. This handful of key threats is sent to management for consideration and evaluation for preemptive work or planning.

Phase III: Issue Confidential Exposure Reports

Figure 8.1 describes the policy and procedure with respect to phase III. Typically these reports are short and to the point, just one or two pages, and printed on only one side of a sheet of paper. They contain extraordinarily valuable management data and input. The distribution of these highly valuable and often highly inflammatory reports is restricted and carefully controlled. Copying is prohibited, and the distributed documents are collected and destroyed after seventy-two hours.

Phase IV: Meet Quarterly for Exposure Review

During phase IV, management discloses its exposure surveillance results and works with others at very high levels in management to ensure that the organization is prepared to eliminate or, at a minimum, compensate for, accommodate, or preempt the impact of these potential threats.

War Stories

Over the course of nearly thirty years of working in devastating civil, criminal, corporate, and government situations, I've amassed a rather amazing collection of scenarios. I call them war stories, and they occupy a significant portion of the file space in my office. Throughout most of my career, as urgent matters have arisen, I have established files for them. Mostly they contain newspaper clippings and magazine writings about these matters. Should these situations arise again in my practice, I can instantly review topical information and immediately begin to apply the lessons of patterns and forecastable circumstances to the questions my clients ask. I also create files for scenarios I believe my clients will be asking about or that will concern me in the future. I use one nearly every day.

Scenario and pattern sensitivity is a state of mind and a discipline one chooses to acquire and use. The benefits are extraordinary. I have literally hundreds and hundreds of war stories that I have been involved with or interested in throughout my career. The following is a partial list of the scenarios I have on file.

Sample List from Jim's War Story Index

Aboveground storage (nuclear fuel)	Adverse investigations
Academic fraud	Agency guidance
Accidents	AIDS
Acquisitions	Air quality violations
Activist action	Aircraft crashes
Acts of God	Ambush interviews
Adversarial interviews	Analysts' presentations
Adverse government action	Angry neighbors

Animal rights	Arsenic contamination
Annual meetings	Asbestos
Anonymous accusers	Attack sites
Anti-corporate activism	

Keep in mind that my career has been devoted to dealing mostly with the extraordinarily bad news of organizations, leaders, and institutions. Your list of scenarios, patterns, and topics of interest will of course conform to your own sphere of influence, current activities, and curiosity.

The Lessons of Pattern and Scenario Awareness

The use of scenarios originated in and until recently was used extensively by the military. The most visible activity in the military's testing of scenario-based readiness is the war game. "War gaming" in business became a more frequent activity in the 1950s and is now a crucial ingredient in making management decisions in most areas of strategic activity. The use of the word *scenario* is an important distinction designed to differentiate between the attitude accompanying a warlike mentality and an aggressive but peaceful approach to solving business and public problems.

The limited discussion in this chapter produces at least five crucial lessons:

Lesson 1: Patterns Are the Foundation of Strategy and Are What Make the Strategist an Intelligent Forecaster

Remember also that scenario planning and pattern analysis are widely accepted management tools. The boss will be ready for you to walk him or her through scenarios and the potential benefits of understanding in advance what can happen. As I have emphasized throughout this book, leadership always benefits from useful, sensible suggestions about what the next steps or increments might be. This is among the greatest contributions trusted strategic advisors can make. Pattern analysis is another key tool for advising the boss on what to do next.

Lesson 2: War Story Files Are One Tool Advisors Can Use to Help the Boss Better Understand a Situation and All Its Ramifications as a Pattern of Events Unfolds

People often see an event or situation in isolation, or see only a small portion of it, missing its full scope. You can put war story files to use at a moment's notice to reveal the big picture and serve as a basis for forecasting the behaviors of key players.

Recently I received a call from someone telling me that I had been referred to him by his legal counsel. A story was going to appear in the newspaper about a senior executive who was soon to be sued for sexual harassment. My caller wanted to know what to do. Having been through several cases, I was able to ask him crucial questions from the start.

"How many executives are involved?" was the first. "Just the one," he said, "and it's going to be a very high-profile situation." My comment was that there's always more than just a single executive, and that it would indeed be a very high-profile situation. Even if only one was engaged in actual harassment, other executives and managers were no doubt aware of this behavior and had allowed it to occur. Those names would surface, and the behavior of those executives and managers would be called into question.

"How many women are involved?" was the next. "Just the one," he answered tentatively. I commented that there has to be more than one. The pattern here is that this behavior involves multiple assaults on multiple individuals.

"Have you located previous female employees to determine why they left, what was said, and what is known about this individual's behavior?" was the third. "These women, though not speaking now due to shame, fear, or embarrassment, will come forward as the story unfolds. Find out how many women are involved."

Then he asked me, "Who have you been talking to?" I honestly answered, "No one. What I'm telling you is the pattern of these events." This organization also tends to think that I am a genius.

Lesson 3: Preemptively Translate Relevant Patterns and Problems into Useful Strategic Tools Management Can Use Before Problems Occur

Maximize the value both of your war stories and your constant scanning of the issues and circumstances affecting other similar organizations. Select the most damaging, dangerous, or destabilizing situations, then translate them into hypothetical scenarios for your company or organization. Here's an example:

Suppose your company has manufacturing and distribution operations in a variety of "back area" locations in various towns and cities, large and small, all across the United States. However, most of your chemical treatment activities and heavy industry processes are located primarily in what are considered lower-income, even poor, areas.

You could someday be the subject of litigation or government action involving "environmental racism." If you were to search on the Web for the terms "environmental racism" or "environmental justice," you'd come across the Environmental Protection Agency's Web site, www.epa.gov, very quickly. If you searched the site for "environmental justice," you'd find the EPA's Federal Register notice of Friday, July 23, 2005, regarding significant revisions in the agency's Environmental Justice Strategy. You may refer to www .whitehouse.gov/ceq/environmentaljustice for guidance under the National Environmental Policy Act. You'd also come across references to the Center for the Study of American Business in Washington, which has published a number of position papers on this subject from a business perspective. Within less than an hour, and even before you seriously reviewed your clippings, you could be extraordinarily knowledgeable on this subject from very important sources, and have one or two brief case studies to back up your impressions, early information, and initial thoughts and recommendations.

Remember, the strategist's job is to provide an adequate explanation for the circumstance being discussed, described, debated, or deliberated; to understand and relate the nature of the threat or opportunity; to provide several options for management to consider and a recommendation for a particular approach, complete with a brief analysis of the negative unintended consequences that could result from the various approaches.

Lesson 4: Focus Most of Your Work on Nonoperating Scenarios

Ninety-five percent of the problems that affect most organizations come directly from day-to-day operations. These are the areas in which there is significant resident expertise. The strategist looks at the other 5 percent, those nonoperating circumstances that present the greatest threat to organizational stability, reputation, and market share and that cause damage that is difficult to repair. Management tends to be at its weakest in responding to nonoperating problems.

The reason nonoperating problems are so difficult for management to cope with is that management schools rarely address them. These situations are often highly emotional and, therefore, irrational, immeasurable, and embarrassing or humiliating besides.

Examples of nonoperating problems include extortion; criminal litigation; employee or community violence; harassment; bullying or assault; activist attacks; Web, blog, and other uncontrollable attacks by antagonists; embarrassing or aggravating situations and allegations; extensive performance criticism; and shareholder activism. When these nonoperating problems are poorly anticipated and handled, it causes the greatest damage to reputation and the greatest threat to the survival of CEOs. When there are victims, these highly emotional situations require special knowledge and expertise, but they also conform to recognizable patterns that if analyzed and understood can aid in the productive resolution of these situations.

Lesson 5: Talking About Patterns Is Often a Powerful Way to Be Memorable

As I noted in Chapter Five, for you to have impact as a strategic advisor, what you say needs to be memorable. A number of years ago, I was working with a small, privately owned timber-harvesting company in northern California. It was a highly controversial operation receiving tremendously negative visibility on a global scale. When the owners of this operation first called me, they told me that they had the best intentions and wanted to make this operation a state-of-the-art, environmentally sustainable laboratory for forestry practices. They then mentioned that despite their good intentions and financial and philosophical ability to execute on their vision, they had terribly underestimated the negative reaction of a whole host of publics. So their question was very simple: "What do we do now?"

I immediately said, "Sell the property—this afternoon." (It was July 4, 1998.) They didn't laugh. So I said, "No, seriously, sell the property this afternoon. Why do you need all the agony, grief, and embarrassment or humiliation such a business and project will bring to you, and in fact probably already has?" Their answer was the same as before. They had the highest of motives in mind, and they wanted to try to make the venture a success.

I went on to describe to them what they would experience, how difficult it would be, and the four things they really had to be ready for. First, they had to be willing to sacrifice much of their substantial wealth to counteract the enormous amount of anti-corporate activism that would be launched against them from many parts of the world. Second, they had to have the stomach for what was going to happen to each one of them—individually, their families, their other businesses, and their relatives. There would be a constant stream of gossip, fabrication, and sensationalism.

Third, it was likely that the most highly visible among them, as well as the richest, would be singled out for special public shaming and naming, and that this is a part of the pattern of attack used by those who oppose them and others in similar situations. Fourth, and the concept toughest of all to internalize, is that this sort of behavior would in all likelihood continue for as long as they owned and worked the property. No matter how much they spent, how successful they were in habitat restoration, saving the salmon, rebuilding the forest floors, and other ecologically important behaviors and activities, they would likely be in the doghouse in a high-profile way with someone, literally forever.

At the end of that phone call, they thanked me for providing such a candid and lucid description of where they had been as well as where they were likely to be going.

They refined the business by recognizing and systematically overcoming the obstacles they knew would be there, and have become one of the more prominent model forestry operations in America, one used as a best-practice example by most environmental groups in the United States and abroad.

Here is just one example of this company's approach. Early on it was evident that to have credibility, the entire organization would have to successfully subject itself to certification by outside criteria, mostly from the opposition. There were two recognized certifying organizations in the company's part of California. Our original discussion was about which of the two to align with to undergo the certification procedures. My immediate response was, "You're going to have to contract with both of them. Whichever one you choose, your opponents and the unchosen certifying organization will consider your approach inadequate and flawed." The company did contract with both certifying organizations, and as part of the process required that both certifiers coordinate their activities. Both organizations did come together to provide independent certification after an extraordinary effort by the company to cooperate. Today the organization is still attacked with some frequency, but its track record improves each day, and that has become its best defense.

Can You Recognize What's Coming Next?

One of the most critical tasks of a trusted advisor, as I have said, is to help leaders figure out what to do next. Understanding the power of patterns can help you do that, because you can often use patterns to forecast what is going to *happen* next. We all tend to think we are unique, our situation special, our challenges exceptional.

My career confirms the fallacy of this kind of thinking, every day. In fact, having been an advisor through all these years and having gone through so many different—mostly adverse—scenarios with organizations and leadership, my takeaway is that thorough study of past scenarios may prevent some aspect of similar future mishaps, but the main benefit is a better, more informed response when something adverse occurs and, more important, better response performance overall.

- Do I have the discipline necessary to collect and organize stories, reports, and case histories of a wide variety of events, companies, people, and situations, and to mine them for even more powerful lessons?
- Will I spend the time to analyze structures, timelines, variables, and key decision points to identify at least the most obvious similarities and threats?
- Can I keep up this practice year after year?

Begin collecting your war stories now. At first the patterns may seem to be less obvious. But over time, you will be amazed at how people will seek you out, thinking you can see the future. Of course, what you will really be seeing are patterns. As Peter Drucker, who saw many trends emerging years before anyone else, once said, "I never predict. I simply look out the window and see what is visible but not yet seen" (quoted in "Peter Drucker's Light Shines On," by Frances Hesselbein, *Leader to Leader*, Spring 2006, no. 40, pp. 4–7).

9

ADVISE CONSTRUCTIVELY

Chapter Outline

Most advisors, early on, tend to give advice in the context of their staff function or personal area of expertise. Typically, staff thinking and decision making are quite different from operational thinking and decision making. To succeed as a trusted strategic advisor to operating executives, you will need to align your thinking patterns and decision-making habits with theirs. This chapter describes a methodology that helps you think and communicate using a more structured and process-driven format. When you use such a format, executives are able to understand your recommendations and see how they relate to ultimate goals and objectives, without their having to do a lot of translating.

How information is structured when presented to management is very important. Whether the solution proposed is bold, obvious common sense, absolutely applicable, or brilliant and creative, managers will absorb advice better if it fits into their processing approach, builds on their intuitive skills and experience, and allows them to assimilate.

The chances of your advice being recognized and utilized increase if you structure it using the same template managers use to make their decisions. The elements of this template are *situation*, *analysis*, *goals*, *options*, *recommendations*, and *justifications*. For decisions that matter, all six template elements will come into play. Omitting or skipping a template element subtracts from the value and completeness of the advice given. In fact, when I learned this approach, it was referred to as the Concept of Completed Action; the source of this name has completely eluded me, but the value of the structured thinking and presentation approach has been a crucial ingredient in my own success.

Talk to time. Be brief. Avoid excessive talking. In addition to respecting the boss's time, brevity is important because concentrated, well-structured information presented verbally or in writing is powerful and more likely to be assimilated and owned by others. Information provided in tabbed manuals and called a Plan is likely to be ignored. Executives base most of their critical decisions on experience and intuition in conjunction with facts and information recently harvested through verbal interaction with colleagues and advisors, usually in a very short span of time.

The Three-Minute Drill

The Three-Minute Drill is a time-sensitive, highly disciplined approach for presenting recommendations. If your strategic recommendations fail to fit this timed structure, go back and rethink, make repairs, and rehearse again. The drill is structured in six steps that impose a useful, sensible management decision-making structure:

Step 1   Situation (60 words)

Describe the nature of the issue, problem, or situation that requires decision, action, or study. This is the factual or perceptual basis for "What we know now," "Why we need to take the boss's time, now, to discuss this," or "This is a new and important topic that we need to talk about, now."

Step 2   Analysis and Assumptions (60 words)

Describe what the situation means, its implications, and perhaps how it threatens, or represents, opportunities. Include one or two key assumptions that validate your analysis. "Here's why it matters."

Managers always need to know the "why," but not in great detail. They are also interested in the intelligence you possess or have gathered that supports your analysis and assumptions.

Step 3   The Goal (60 words)

State the task to be accomplished (sometimes the reason or purpose for accomplishing it) or the goal or destination to be reached and why. "This is where we are headed."

Goals provide focus. Useful goals are understandable, achievable, brief, positive, and time and deadline sensitive.

Step 4   Options (150 words)

Provide at least three response options to address the situation as presented and analyzed. Option one is to do nothing (the 0 percent solution); option two is to do something (the 100 percent solution); and option three is to do something more (the 125 percent solution). Providing multiple options is what will keep you at the table and avoids the high-risk strategy of making a single recommendation, which can be torpedoed by a single question. We'll discuss the nature of these options just a bit later in this chapter.

Step 5   Recommendation (60 words)

Be prepared to make a specific choice among the options you presented. You will usually make your recommendation on the basis of which option will cause the fewest unintended negative consequences. This is where you earn your paycheck.

Many times I have heard advisors offer reasonable options, but when the boss ultimately asks the question— "What is the first thing I should do?" "What are the next steps?" or "Of the three recommendations, which would you choose and why?"—far too often the response from the proposer is, "Gee, boss, that's a good question, and I need to think about that," putting an end to the advisor's usefulness in the discussion, at least in this round, and undercutting other advice as well.

Being ready with a recommendation and supporting information every time is your passport to the inner circle.

Step 6   Justification (60 words)

Every management decision or action has intended and unintended consequences that can be forecast. Inadequate provision for consequences is what can sometimes sabotage an otherwise useful strategy.

As I mentioned in step 5, when I think of consequences and strategy, I generally try to identify the solution option with the fewest negative intended or unintended consequences.

Strive to provide advice in this 450-word format (three minutes). It is powerful, it conserves management time, and, coupled with the discipline of suggesting three action options, it will get you invited back to the table again and again. Anyone who can spontaneously provide three decision options on the spot, every time, as opposed to whining and griping, is extraordinarily valuable. Keep this up, and you could become the boss's first call when it matters.

The Options

My preference is to talk about doing *nothing* before anyone else does. My experience is that when the lawyers talk about doing nothing, the discussion sometimes ends right at that point. The discussion only resumes when some catastrophic development or unexpected adverse situation occurs. My sense is that I'm often in the best position to discuss the impacts and costs of doing nothing better than any other staff function. Certainly human resources, finance, strategic planning, security, and IT can also address the circumstance, but on issues that matter, where there are victims and serious visibility risks, doing nothing can be extremely costly. This is a valid strategy option and needs to be discussed and debated. The option to do *something* is crucial. Most problems, although benefiting from some initial lack of action, do require some input of energy, resources, talent, and decision making if they are to be resolved. Having an action recommendation assists the boss in that crucial area called "what to do next."

Doing *something more* is the notion that resolving problems, especially those that are disturbing, stressful, or destructive to an organization, may require more than a minimally adequate response. Doing something more means going beyond meeting the letter of the law or the minimum, and taking additional steps that will further enhance the organization's reputation, assist those adversely affected, or repair a previous mistake. This approach is often the difference between a leader's solution and a manager's solution. Managers address only the known visible elements of a given situation. The leader's vision is to look more globally at the benefits of a larger effort or response concept.

Sometimes I'm asked, "What if there is only one appropriate action for the boss to take? Everyone knows it, even the boss knows it, but there's resistance. Would it be possible to use this technique so that after you discuss doing nothing, you offer something you know the boss should do, and then something so ridiculous that the boss's choice is clearly obvious?" My experience has been that the more outlandish the suggestion you make, the more likely it is that the boss will select it. And, of course, because you suggested it, you'll be put in charge of making it work. That is a very risky strategy. Let the process of executive decision making play out. Offer options that are useful, sensible, and appropriate, options you can ethically and professionally execute. Help the process of decision making move ahead through your remaining analysis and suggestions.

It's the boss's watch and the boss's career. That leaves the decision ultimately up to the boss. Whatever the boss chooses, you'll be there to help and advise.

Doing Something Badly

My father used to say, "When in doubt, do something," but over the years I've learned there is a right way and wrong way to do something. Some years ago I was visiting a large international retailer on a product-related problem. While I was there, I was pulled into a meeting involving a serious customer situation. One of the retailer's computers had hiccuped and added anywhere from $2 to $200 to the balance due for the monthly statements of more than fifty thousand customers. The glitch had just been discovered, and the executive meeting I was pulled into was to debate how or whether to notify customers. After listening to the conversation for a few minutes, I shook my head negatively. This got some attention. The executives turned and asked me what they should do, in my opinion. I said, "First of all, in my household, it's my wife, Barbara, who manages the books, writes the checks, and maintains all household accounts and relationships. If her checkbook or any of the accounts she balances every month is off by even a dime, she is unable to sleep until she can resolve the matter. Potentially, you have created thousands of sleepless customers out there, trying to figure out what the heck happened and why there is a difference between their bills and their receipts. The longer you wait to inform customers, the more damaging the consequences are likely to be."

Then I suggested that they consider drafting a highly personal letter from a senior executive, perhaps even the CEO, apologizing for the error, explaining what happened and what's being done about it, asking people's patience while the matter was being corrected, and describing specifically how customers would be notified about the credits or corrections on their bills. I further suggested that they include coupons with each letter of apology that were some multiple of the amounts in the error. Because every customer involved was known, as was the amount of each error, this calculation could be done easily. For example, a person with a $2 error would receive $25 in coupons; a $10 error, $40 in coupons; up to a $200 error, $1,000 in coupons. This is where I lost them. You would have thought I was offering a solution so off-the-wall that it would break this company financially. It was a $30 billion company.

My suggestion triggered a very high-volume discussion, especially about granting $25 gift certificates for $2 errors. One executive argued that if we carried the ratio through to the $200 error, "why, the company would be paying tens of thousands of dollars for a simple mistake in customers' bills, which was caused by a computer. No one in this room is responsible," he said.

My point was, "It's not the $200 error customers who are going to sue the company; it's the $2 error customers who will sue. It isn't the big mistakes that are so offensive; it's the little, mindless stumbles, fumbles, and bumbles that really irritate and frustrate people." The $20 victims would make the most powerful plaintiffs because they make the most dramatic and captivating victims.

The executives thanked me, and I went back to work on the product-related problem I was originally brought in to help handle. A number of months later, I read in the paper of a class action lawsuit being filed against this retailer by some fourteen thousand customers who had mysterious small errors in their bills. It turns out that the company had decided to send a perfunctory letter addressed "Dear Customer" and signed by a "Director of Customer Satisfaction." The signature on the letter was of an individual whose name I didn't recognize.

When I inquired about the lawsuit and the letter, my contact at the company reviewed the circumstances for me. The lawyers had prevailed, and a letter was sent to customers that included nothing more than, "Computers made a mistake on your bill in the amount of ___," and "this will be corrected within 120 days." But it was the company's "apology" that was so startling. The letter said, "If this mistake created problems for you, we are sorry, but this was an isolated incident caused by a computer problem that was well beyond our control."

Here's the kicker. When I asked about the gentleman who signed the letter, executives at the company told me it was a fictitious person. The policy in the credit department was that when letters of this nature are being sent to customers, they are signed by a fictitious person to protect employees against retribution by angry customers.

I think there were several more large-scale lawsuits that followed this class action. Maybe doing nothing is safer sometimes, but only rarely. It's never safer to do something stupid, arrogant, and unbelievably callous, as this company did. As I recall, the majority of plaintiffs suffered losses or errors of less than $50.

Providing three doable options every time you offer advice will draw people to you for counsel. Anyone who can come up with three constructive approaches (remember that doing nothing can be constructive) to any given situation, on the spot, is a person of great value. This is one of the key ingredients of being a trusted strategic advisor.

Providing a range of possible courses of action also helps defeat another powerful force that operates in management: the desire to kill anything new or different and keep things just as they are. This is the area where intuitive thinkers fail frequently. They focus on the silver bullet, the big idea. If you have only one recommendation and there are even a couple of questions about it, the idea will die, and you'll be out of the discussion from that point.

Death by Question

The corporate execution method for new and big ideas is what I call death by question, usually at the hands of other staff functions. Suppose you have a wonderful idea for solving a serious corporate problem. Your idea is innovative, interesting, and somewhat different from the usual approaches. Rather than shooting your idea down by saying it won't work, it's not possible, it doesn't fit the culture, and all those other negatives, the execution begins with a series of questions. The first question might be, "Have you run this by finance to determine the fiscal impact?" You probably haven't, which means your idea is now bleeding from a serious wound. Then comes killer question two: "Has human resources had a chance to review the impact on employees, service levels, and local operating structures?" It's another bullet, of slightly larger caliber. But they've saved the best and biggest bullet for last: "If you were given the go-ahead with your proposal, could you finance it completely out of your own budget this year?" Well, by now it feels like your idea is lying in a bloody puddle on the floor, and you are out of arguments and out of the game.

The concept of options is powerful, because it can withstand death by question. You may be shot down on one part of your idea, perhaps even a good part of the second concept, but it's rare that even a large group can shoot down three suggestions. Some fragment of your thinking is going to remain on the table. This means you will undoubtedly be there through the entire discussion.

Keep in mind that the ultimate decision may hardly resemble anything that you proposed, but as a trusted strategic advisor, you're still there, you're still in the game, you're still ready to offer additional options beyond the first set. This is one of the crucial values the trusted strategic advisor provides: a useful, restrained, but productive attitude that fosters ideas for tomorrow and helps move whole issues and circumstances to new levels of understanding and resolution.

Learn and Use This Management Decision-Making Structure

Each of the six management decision-making components just discussed (situation, analysis, goals, options, recommendations, and justifications) has three powerful common elements:

1. **Factual basis.** You are working with what is actually known, can be counted on, trusted, seen, or measured. In the early

stages of change, important situations are so often "underfac-
tualized" that logical decision making seems difficult, if not
impossible. When you're giving advice in this format, facts
matter. Examples will help. But management will need to see
sufficient information to provide measurable or conclusive
evidence of progress.

2. **Real-time value.** For issues that matter, ideally the gap in
   time between decision and action is very small. The larger
   the gap, the greater the likelihood that significant changes
   in the facts surrounding the situation may make a portion or
   all of the action decisions faulty, or at least less than optimal.

3. **Outcome focus.** Strategic decision making is always about
   moving toward the future. The past can only be reimagined,
   rewritten, and reinterpreted. It is what it was. Focusing
   on outcomes helps set the past aside and deal in terms of
   tomorrow. This is the destiny-driven approach. It leads
   to productive, focused decision making. Use it and you'll
   get to help managers at every level make better strategic
   decisions. In fact, use this approach and you will find yourself being called in earlier and asked to stay longer.

Exhibit 9.1, the Three-Minute Drill Worksheet, fulfills two
important functions. First, it serves as a guide to learning how to
use the Three-Minute Drill as a format for thinking and making
decisions. Keep in mind the word counts and the purpose of each
of the six elements. Second, you can use this format on your
computer or as a handwritten form and worksheet that you bring
to meetings to develop options on the spot.

Exhibit 9.2, the Best Option Process Worksheet, is a differ-
ent format for achieving the same goal as the Three-Minute Drill
(Exhibit 9.1)—it is a highly disciplined approach for refining and
presenting recommendations—but one that I find works better if
I'm going through this process with a small or large group. The Best
Option Process Worksheet is meant to serve as a discussion support

Exhibit 9.1 Three-Minute Drill Worksheet

Issue, Question, Situation _____

Situation

(60 words)
Briefly describe the nature of the issue, problem, or situation that requires decision, action, or study. "This is the subject and here's what we know now."

Analysis and Assumptions

(60 words)
A description of what the situation means, what its implications are, and how it threatens or presents an opportunity to the organization. "Here's why it matters."

The Goal

(60 words)
A clear, concise statement of the task to be accomplished (sometimes the reason or purpose for accomplishing it), the target to be reached, and when. "Our destination."

(Continued)

Exhibit 9.1 (Continued)

Options

(150 words)
Provide at least
three response
options to address
the situation as
presented and analyzed:

1. Do nothing

2. Do something

3. Do something more

Recommendation

(60 words)
Make a specific choice
among the options you
presented. Be ready with a
recommendation and
supporting information
every time because the
boss is going to ask
you for one.

Justification

(60 words)
Briefly describe the
reactions or circumstances
that could arise resulting
from the options you
suggested, including that
of doing nothing. Identify
the solution option with
the fewest negative
intended or unintended
consequences.

Exhibit 9.2 Best Option Process Worksheet

This worksheet is designed to capture the Three-Minute Drill approach. The total amount of time to present concepts to management, in the order shown below, should be approximately three minutes, or 450 words or less. Always maximize the value of time spent with executives, from their perspective.

Date:_____

Problem: Describe clearly, directly, and briefly

_____

_____

Urgency: Why now

_____

_____

Outcome Desired: What's the goal

_____

_____

Solution Options: Identify the alternatives

1. _____

   _____

2. _____

   _____

3. _____

   _____

Best Option: Recommend the first-choice action (also indicate the second-best option)

_____

_____

Reasons (Consequences): Justify your choice; indicate consequences avoided and achieved

1. _____

   _____

2. _____

   _____

template; it's designed to help structure, contain, and facilitate the process of developing options and the related information.

The message of both Exhibit 9.1 and Exhibit 9.2 is that at the rate of 450 words per recommendation, you're talking to time and should be able to get your recommendations on one side of a single sheet of paper. This is always an excellent strategy when providing written materials you want your boss to act on.

More Strategic Advice-Giving Tools

To supplement the Three-Minute Drill and to help give additional information in a management context, there are three other highly effective tools you might choose to use:

Timelines

One of the most strategic documents for making recommendations is the timeline driven by the calendar or a clock, depending on the time frames being considered. I've made the point time and again that management is about tomorrow. Any recommendations that fit in the sequence of getting things done, making decisions, or choosing alternatives are more important than other activities. Timelines can accommodate a variety of different activities that are all moving forward at the same time but at different velocities. For example, when locating or siting a new building, plant, or branch office, there can be literally dozens of timelines at work and interacting with each other. The list would include design and architecture; site acquisition and public permit acquisition; public affairs and policy chains; planning and communications; legal and regulatory issues, permissions, oversight, and restrictions; recruiting locally for available positions; occupancy checklists and requirements—you get the idea.

The value of timelines is that if one element of a particular schedule of activities slips, slides, is eliminated, or is completed early, it is easy to adjust the timeline, and the overall thinking and strategy are less affected, if at all.

Prioritized Lists

Another extremely helpful technique is to prioritize actions, events, decisions, and outcomes. Virtually any list of activities, ideas, or concepts that is prioritized is strategically helpful. As discussed throughout this book, a key activity for a strategic advisor is helping the boss establish priorities, figure out what to do next, and understand the range of options for accomplishing the next steps. Helping the boss set priorities is helping set the agenda for the entire organization.

Flowcharts

Another powerful communications tool for advisors is the flowchart. There are many varieties of flowcharts, but the more complex the idea, concept, or recommendation you are describing, the more valuable it becomes to develop a prioritized picture of actions, steps, and decisions.

Operations people are accustomed to reading flowcharts, which are in essence illustrations of process thinking. So next time, rather than writing a complicated memo of recommendations, try drawing the recommendation as a sequence of events from beginning to end, designed as a picture of decisions and actions moving ahead in an organized, prioritized fashion. A single flowchart, generally on one side of one sheet of paper, is worth at least a notebook full of words and tabs.

10

SHOW THE BOSS HOW TO USE YOUR ADVICE

Chapter Outline

Giving Constructive Advice

    Goal focus

    Long-term thinking

    Process orientation

    Strategic relevance

Giving Advice Effectively

    Be positive

    Eliminate criticism as a coaching and advising practice

Urge prompt action

Focus on outcomes

Be carefully reflective

Be an incrementalist

Be pragmatic

Advice Givers and Advice Takers

Be a Strategic Force

In his groundbreaking book *Taking Advice* (2006), Dan Ciampa talks about the "attitudes and behaviors of great advice takers" (p. 139). Among the insights he offers on this topic is his discussion of the relationship that needs to be established between the boss and the trusted advisor. From the boss's perspective, he talks about four behaviors bosses tend to look for: practicality, added value, dependability, and commitment. He actually refers to these as relationship tests because both the advisor *and* the leader must pass them together.

    Practicality, according to Ciampa, puts the advisor in a position to give useful, doable, achievable advice because instructions, goals, and expected behaviors are clear. The added-value test refers to the dialogue between the advisor and the leader. This test is passed when "at the end of each substantive meeting the leader knows something more valuable than he did before, or is more clearheaded about how to proceed" (p. 156). The dependability test is essentially the "Can I trust this person?" question. Does the advisor spontaneously provide useful, helpful information as expected? And, at the same time, is the leader forthcoming and responsive to the advice being given by the advisor in a tone that is respectful and helpful?

With regard to the commitment test, Ciampa poses two defining questions from the boss's perspective:

1. Does the advisor genuinely seem interested in the kinds of problems I have?
2. Does the advisor seem to care about my success?

Clearly, if the answer to these questions is yes, the leader and the advisor are more likely to develop a successful relationship, and the leader is likely to become a better advice taker.

Aside from practicality, added value, dependability, and commitment, there are other habits and behaviors of trusted advisors that foster, nurture, and maintain this spirit of collaborative dialogue, resulting in actions and behaviors on the part of leaders that reflect the value of the shared relationship. Once a trusted strategic advisor proves his or her dependability, the first imperative is to teach leaders how to use the advice they are given.

Giving Constructive Advice

Being constructive has a special meaning when it comes to being a trusted strategic advisor. It means avoiding, in fact, eliminating, the use of criticism as an advisory technique. Replace that negative approach by always providing helpful, positive assistance. But being constructive is actually even deeper and broader than that. One of the ingredients of genuine leadership is the ability to hear many voices, then to choose the most interesting, helpful, important, or powerful elements of those voices and fashion a new structure of ideas, decisions, and actions. It has struck me, over the years, that the "attitude" of the information received determines how useful or acceptable it will be in resolving issues and helping move mission, goals, projects, strategies, and people toward the future. One of the key disciplines of a successful advisor is the ability to provide information with the right tone, the right structure, and the right intention. Sharing your intentions with those you counsel is also essential to your success. Rather than waiting for your boss to notice, take the time to explain the what, why, how, when, and where of your advising style, and the techniques you use.

Constructive approaches have four elements.

Goal Focus

As Stephen Covey would say, plan with the end in mind. Have a destination before you start the journey, and understand the outcome you seek to achieve before you begin. More good intentions perish for want of a clearly defined destination than for almost any other reason. A focus on the goal tends to reduce the wandering generality tendency and to force people to focus on more meaningful specifics, more meaningful actions that construct the desired outcomes. If the goal is missing, you and the boss are going nowhere.

Long-Term Thinking

It's true that the vast majority of advice sought and given relates to matters occurring generally within a current budget or fiscal period. The strategic advisor's perspective, like that of the leaders they advise, is always one of looking at today's decisions in terms of their consequences for tomorrow. A wonderfully important achievement today may actually be somewhat cumbersome to explain in the future, when such activity can be viewed from an entirely different and perhaps negative perspective. When we embrace long-term thinking, we are saying that everything we do today (everything that matters, anyway) affects tomorrow. We must at least think about those impacts and outcomes and advise more carefully in the present if we want to have better outcomes in the future.

Process Orientation

As noted elsewhere, senior managers generally prefer a process approach. They've learned that processes with well-thought-out elements and phases that can be taught, replicated, and evaluated will yield results of more uniform quality. Any advice you give needs to be structured using a process-driven format, or it will be largely ignored, misunderstood, or disregarded.

Strategic Relevance

Among all the ingredients of being a trusted strategic advisor, being strategic is the most challenging. So often, people in staff functions have difficulty relating to corporate strategy. They talk a good game, even use a lot of management vocabulary, but their minds simply fail to function in a strategic way, and they produce advice that is too shallow or only of limited use. To a certain extent, this is expected. Each staff function has its applicability to achieving organizational or leadership goals. Yet as we've seen, among the major lessons of the seven-discipline approach is that these disciplines aid the trusted advisor in maintaining relevance to management.

Giving Advice Effectively

Aside from the actual quality of your advice, how you communicate that advice plays a major role in ensuring that the boss can and will listen to it and act on it. The seven approaches suggested here help achieve this goal.

Be Positive

In business conversation, when someone says something with which you disagree, you may be inclined to respond with something like, "You're wrong," "That's incorrect," "You don't know what you're talking about," "It's simply not done that way," or some similar negative comment. You may then go on to explain what is correct or how you really do things, but your listener is still dealing with the insult of your negative language. This makes it almost impossible for him or her to hear your constructive language. Negative comments almost always put other people on the defensive even though our comments are important, positive, and constructive.

The Bad News Eradicator is a little exercise I invented in which I present a list of common negative phrases and then challenge my client to turn them into positives. The full-length version of this exercise is many pages long. (My collection of negative comments currently numbers more than five hundred.) Learning to use positive language is a discipline and a matter of personal practice. This exercise will help you discipline yourself to use positive language in real time, before you've let negative wording slip out. The following list is a tiny sample of negative-to-positive transformations. Remember, there are lots of options for each positive response.

Bad News Eradicator Sample

Negative	Positive
"We don't do it that way."	"Here's the way we do it . . ."
"That's not our style."	"Here are important elements of our style . . ."
"The boss won't buy it."	"Here's what the boss has bought in the past; here's what he [she] may buy in the future . . ."
"That's a lie."	"If you check your facts and assumptions, you may come to a different conclusion."
	"Using the same analysis, we came up with a different, more positive result."

The lesson is this: your use of negative language constricts, obstructs, and damages your relationship with other people. Eradicate or eliminate negative and emotional words, and you become far more powerful and in control of almost any situation. Your positive approach blocks or defeats those who are negative. Most arguments, misunderstandings, confusion, and aggressive behavior are triggered by negative words, phrases, and attitudes. In situations of confrontation and controversy, at least one side of the argument needs the negativity of the other to continue operating effectively and pushing the argument forward. Eliminate that negative energy, and the participants can actually make progress or seek a more peaceful resolution.

Eliminate Criticism as a Coaching and Advising Practice

Using criticism as a teaching and change technique leads to very bad results. The people you advise are hurt or confused. Negative advice often leads to even more negative behavior. Constructive criticism is an oxymoron. Angry, negative language leads to a future with angry, negative people. Positive outcomes require positive language.

For example, recently I received a call from a friend who was in charge of evaluating the performance of the new minister in her church after a year's service. She had put together a brief letter to members of the congregation asking that they provide some criticism. I believe she used the words "constructive criticism" of the minister's performance. She mailed seven hundred letters, and she received more than five hundred responses containing an average of three comments each.

The feedback was devastating. If you added up all the criticisms, there was no way this minister could possibly continue in the job and survive emotionally. Most of the criticisms were negatives; many reflected individual misunderstandings, and almost none reflected knowledge of the scope of the congregation's mission or the daily activities required of the minister as the congregation's leader. The criticisms boiled down to negative personal commentary. (Ask anyone to critique your appearance, preparation, proposal, presentation, personality . . . anything, and you are guaranteed to receive dozens of minor negative comments, most of which you can't use or implement even if you wanted to. Most critiques elicit negative, unhelpful information; they are irritating and often embarrassing.)

My friend's problem was, of course, that she had to share the criticism with the minister. The mail came through his office, there was lots of it, and he was very curious. Because this mail was so negative, she needed a good way to handle the information and avoid hurting his feelings. Although the congregation really liked this man and wanted him to stay, not even a minister could likely withstand this level of personal criticism.

I told her about a lesson I learned early in my career from Chester Burger, who is now retired, but who for many decades was one of America's most famous, beloved, and influential business communications consultants. He had faced similar situations inside corporations. Rather than criticizing past performance, he would ask each client executive to make one positive, constructive suggestion about what he or she might do to achieve the goals of the organization. This technique is incredibly powerful and positive.

My friend wrote a simple note to the seven hundred congregation members thanking them for participating in what she now called "phase one" of the pastor's assessment and asking that they participate in "phase two" by suggesting up to three things the pastor could do in the next six to nine months to move the congregation into the future.

After this conversation, I lost track of my friend for just over a year. When I saw her next at a business meeting, I asked her about the minister's health and demeanor. She immediately shared that they had received a total of twelve suggestions. My friend did go back to the minister, in all honesty, and showed him both the first assessments and then the follow-up correspondence. The minister

not only stayed but also initiated implementation of every suggestion in the first ninety days.

The lesson is this: you have the power to structure and control
productive discussions and debate. If you want constructive results,
seek and insist on constructive suggestions. There will be very few,
but they will be useful. If you make positive, constructive suggestions, you automatically control and therefore powerfully manage
how decisions are made.

Urge Prompt Action

Speed is the great detoxifier and emotion controller. Acting
quickly defeats or preempts the actions of critics. Prompt apology can all but eliminate litigation. Speedy decisions and actions
help you outrun the competition and those who love to live
in the past. The longer it takes a senior manager or leader to
respond to a problem, the more complex and costly the solution
becomes. In this day and age, every leader, and certainly every
trusted advisor, should be prepared for surprise to the point where
they can avoid time-consuming meetings and delays by exercis-
ing preauthorized responses to attacks, problems, instability, fear,
mistakes, or errors.

Over the years, I've learned that whether it's an activist group,
angry employees, upset neighbors, or jealous competitors who
appear to be outsmarting us, the way to win, the way to move
things forward, the way to stay in charge is to act now and do it
now . . . every time.

This often means making smaller decisions and acting on them
more quickly.

- Answer it now. If there are questions, get the answers and get
  them now.
- Ask it now. Rather than waiting for someone else to ask the
  serious question, ask first to get the answers out there.

- Challenge it now. If it's wrong, correct it. If it's legitimate, act on it. If it's an alternative worth considering, decide and act.
- If you know it's going to be a problem, act now to eliminate the cause.
- Fix it now. If it's broken, move to repair it; if it's breaking down, move to shore it up.

The lesson is this: those who act promptly, who do it now, are ahead of the competition and produce fewer new critics, enemies, and naysayers. Prompt action often foils the opposition's most carefully laid plans and can defeat almost any critic, while better controlling the situation.

The linear thinkers may criticize you for this. "Move that fast, and you'll make more mistakes." Mistakes will be made anyway. Deferring them to some other time only delays success and makes relatively simple problems even worse. Make the inevitable mistakes early. Fix them faster and move on more successfully. You'll just make different new mistakes earlier. This is how actual progress is achieved.

Focus on Outcomes

Always focus on a goal. In 1995, I was deeply involved in negotiations between some powerful anti-corporate forces: groups of labor unions, church groups, and NGOs. The issues were extraordinarily compelling and divisive; they were in the news and to some extent in the streets. The challenge was to find a way to sit down face-to-face, put these matters in some perspective, and develop a plan of action.

Fortunately, someone suggested that we meet with a minister in Brooklyn Heights, New York, just across the East River from Manhattan. He was reputed to have the personal presence and an unusual strategy to manage such a politically charged confrontation.

We met in his living room in December. This huge, jovial man greeted us warmly, asked us sit down together in front of a roaring fire, listen to some music, and be quiet for a few minutes.

He then set just one ground rule for the day's work: the discussion was to be entirely outcome focused. This meant that whatever happened between us prior to entering his living room was out of bounds (disagreements, arguments, behaviors, truth, fiction, and lies). The past was completely off-limits to our current discussion. If this ground rule was a problem, he promised to end the discussions and bid us a pleasant day.

It's crucial to understand just how powerful this concept is. Fundamentally, it recognizes that everyone owns yesterday, last week, last month, and last year from his or her own point of reference. That ownership is permanent. Even given a limitless amount of discussion, the past will remain as it was, owned by those who were there.

But no one owns the future—the next fifteen minutes, the next day, the next week, the next month, the next year. Therefore, when we choose to be outcome focused, we are choosing to enter, live, and build a future together.

Now back to Brooklyn Heights. Each time anyone began a discussion supported by something from the past, our host would halt the discussion and refocus it on tomorrow. It was tough for these real-time adversaries to stick to the process, but by 4:30 that afternoon on December 15, 1995, we had negotiated and signed a one-page agreement. Those who signed it, and the businesses and organizations they represented, still live by it today.

The lesson is this: focus on tomorrow and take from yesterday only the positive, useful, constructive elements and ideas that can move the process forward, promptly. There will be very few, if any. Focusing on the future allows you to build tomorrow free of the problems, misunderstandings, and crippling assumptions of the past.

Bonus lesson: applying this single concept will substantially cut meeting and discussion time. A good portion of most meetings is spent explaining to those who weren't at the last meeting what went on and what has yet to be done. Then it's necessary to explain because some of those who attended the last meeting have a very different perception of what went on than you do. What little time remains is used to get something done and move ahead.

Skip yesterday. Go to tomorrow and save tons of time. Tomorrow can start only when today is over. Todays that are governed by yesterday only cause more problems and may even prevent a successful tomorrow. Outcome focus saves precious time, reduces mistakes and misunderstandings, and acts as a positive force for moving ahead.

You get to the future faster by starting there.

Be Carefully Reflective

In Chapter Eight, I emphasized the importance of examining past patterns. Because patterns repeat themselves, they can lead to a powerful scenario planning process. How does that jibe with my advice about being goal oriented and always focused on tomorrow? The point is this: consult the past selectively and carefully, with a specific purpose—that being to strengthen your advice about the future. It can be useful to reflect on certain past situations and how others have dealt with similar issues, but remember: the boss needs advice on what to do next. Seek only useful, positive lessons from the past, if you go there at all. Valuable positive lessons from the past are very rare. Studying the past to predict the future can be extremely risky. Looking backwards, like walking backwards, is the opposite of looking forward.

One of the silliest aphorisms one hears about the past is that hindsight is 20/20. In my experience, foresight is almost always confused, mistaken, and flawed in many respects, and needs to be reinterpreted constantly. Hindsight can only be as good as its flawed foresight.

History does repeat itself unless we take specific action to eliminate the ingredients for a similar problem to occur in the future.

Be an Incrementalist

Being an incrementalist actually prepares the leader and the organization to watch for and recognize big breakthroughs. Such breaks are as much a matter of luck as anything. Luck is limited. Luck actually comes most often to those who are relentlessly incremental in their personal progress every day. As Louis Pasteur so famously said, "Chance favors the prepared mind."

The most credible advisors are those who relentlessly and intentionally

- Grow and learn every day.
- Help those they serve to achieve some positive incremental progress every single day.
- Identify and talk about what gets achieved every day (any incremental step accomplished that moves a project or goal forward) or the positive increments they learn from those they work with, supervise, or lead.
- Assess continuously what they've learned, then teach that learning to others.

Be Pragmatic

Your credibility rests more on what you are actually able to accomplish than on any series of goals or concepts you may choose to announce but only partially or completely fail to achieve. Pragmatic advisors focus on what's doable.

One of the more interesting stories about pragmatism appears in Jack Welch's book *Straight from the Gut*. He had just finished listening to nuclear engineers decide how they were going to begin selling three nuclear reactors per year in the United States, and how doing so would save this General Electric division.

After listening for an hour, Welch thoughtfully responded that no matter how good the intentions were, nuclear reactors were not going to be sold again in the United States in their lifetime, that they needed to focus on something else, and that perhaps servicing existing nuclear facilities would be a more pragmatic approach. GE is now tops in its category of servicing and proposing nuclear facilities, primarily outside the United States. Welch and his team knew how to be pragmatic.

The lesson for strategic advisors is this: a pragmatist relentlessly matches rhetoric with reality. Help each person achieve his or her goals in ways the person can recognize from his or her own perspective. To paraphrase Dale Carnegie: help the other guy get what he wants, from his perspective, and he'll help you get what you want, from your perspective.

Pragmatism is saying and doing things that "make sense." Achievement results from what gets done.

Advice Givers and Advice Takers

As you seek to give effective advice, it is useful to remember Dan Ciampa's point, cited at the beginning of this chapter, that both leaders *and* advisors must work to make the advising relationship effective. As Ciampa notes, effective leaders know how to solicit and take advice. But sometimes bosses simply don't want to hear the advice they receive, or resent being put in a position where they need to ask for advice. Some advice is just very hard to accept. Recent business scandals really have CEOs on the defensive because they are increasingly being measured on their morality, their belief systems, their commitment to society, and to some degree on the perception of honesty and integrity they convey and support. They haven't been trained to meet these standards, and never expected to be. Public attitude surveys consistently demonstrate that the public is fed up with the apparent greed and amorality of corporate leadership. The more hard-bitten executives call these public expectations sissy stuff, and even Goody Two-Shoes or Sunday School stuff. They resent being given advice along these lines, and resent even more the compliance oversight they are subject to as a result.

A client company some years ago was indicted for dozens of felonies, implicated in at least two deaths, and charged with conspiracy involving the alteration of medical products without FDA approval—criminal matters all. It took six years, but when the matter finally came to trial, the company pleaded guilty. (I wrote the allocution statement for the current CEO, the replacement of the former CEO, who was indicted and acquitted and who subsequently retired.) In addition, I helped the law firm develop the plea agreement and its very onerous restrictions and sanctions. (The company paid what was at the time the highest fine ever levied by the government in a FDA product-tampering case.)

I was deeply involved in developing the revisions to the code of conduct, the integrity provisions, and some of the compliance standards and enforcement procedures. The law firm allowed me to present my own work in connection with theirs to senior management. The goal was to review the guidelines as laid out in the plea agreement, and to discuss how the company was going to be operated in the foreseeable future.

When the presentation was finished and we asked for questions, the CEO of the company, who never really liked me anyway, said, "Lukaszewski, whenever you are around here, it seems a little bit like Sunday School." My response was, "Well, Bill, if my company just pleaded guilty to dozens of felonies, I'd think a little Sunday School might be in order." Everybody but Bill laughed. Bill's term as CEO lasted only another eight months. Then he was gone. I have continued as a consultant to the company.

The lesson is this: some bosses resent taking advice, even if they know they have to follow it. Sometimes, because of the boss's attitude, bad relationships continue. Building a good relationship is, as Ciampa noted, a shared responsibility. You also need a leader who seeks advice in good faith. If the person you are advising avoids dealing in good faith, why would you want to stay?

Be a Strategic Force

Giving advice effectively is a strategic force that helps drive individuals, organizations, cultures, and societies forward every day. The discipline of being intentionally constructive and maintaining a relentlessly positive approach helps those you advise be more receptive to the help you offer.

How will you know when you have become a strategic force as an advisor? There are some indicators. You'll be invited to share your opinions at higher levels within your organization. As a matter of daily routine, you'll be able to articulate what is truly important, useful, and helpful to others. Overall, you'll notice that the more strategic your advice, from your boss's perspective, the more important the responsibilities, tasks, and questions your work will involve. This may mean moving to more important work than that which you're currently doing. It may mean evaluating your current environment and determining whether or not you can become a leadership force within the situation in which you currently find yourself.

Leaders automatically tend to assess their own performance each day. They ask themselves several questions. This is a personal discipline that ensures that even their most frustrating day is rewarding and important. As an advisor, you should ask yourself the same questions:

- What did I learn today?
- How can I apply that learning to something I'm currently working on or something I want to work on?
- What did others learn from me today?
- How many times today did someone tell me that they heard me quoted in a meeting they attended and that people were inspired to move ahead?
- What have I improved in some way for someone else today?

Conclusion

You Are the Table

Lucky for you, the "table" everyone talks about getting to (and at which every top operating executive actually dreads being) is a myth. Yes, there are meetings, seminars, Web seminars, conferences, teleconferences, videoconferences, task forces, study groups, working groups, podcast briefings, executive teams, work teams, collaborative wiki Web sites, advisory committees, and boards—all populated by well-meaning, highly motivated, energetic individuals working to get things done. Although each of these groups can play a useful, often necessary role in the advancement of various organizational and business objectives, the meaningful breakthroughs are achieved through other means.

Significant progress and the crystallization of leadership aspirations are usually the work of trusted individual advisors interacting with a leader or leadership group within an organization and having a constructive, measurable impact. This is because, if you are one of these trusted individuals, you are the table. You bring the table with you. When you are in the room, the table is full. When you study the significant decisions leaders make, when you study successful organizations and the actions of those who lead them, you find that these top individuals seek out those with special insight, those with special skills, and, individually rather than collectively, those who provide the crucial information increments these leaders need to make significant decisions and progress.

The philosophy behind this book is that being a trusted strategic advisor is an individual achievement and responsibility. The truth is that senior executives directly and intentionally choose those whom they trust to advise them on the issues that matter.

Senior managers look for expertise, insight, wisdom, loyalty, commitment, and specialized knowledge as preliminary credentials for the position of trusted advisor. If the only thing you have to offer is communications advice, HR advice, legal advice, security advice, marketing advice, or financial advice, then, quite logically, you will be called in only to provide that kind of help. The questions asked of you will be limited to your specific area of expertise. Once you undertake to achieve the disciplines of the trusted strategic advisor—a permanent personal commitment, as described in the chapters of this book—you will experience significant individual rewards, such as access, influence, and impact.

What matters is the constructive connection between the leader and the advisor—the enhanced understanding and reliability that this relationship establishes, fosters, and nurtures. You are the table because no matter how many well-meaning individuals are jammed into a room, the likelihood of something productive occurring, from the boss's perspective or as compared to your meeting with the boss alone, goes down dramatically with each additional voice present.

Most of my career has been spent working primarily in the fields of crisis communication management and response, leadership building, reputation recovery, and strategy. One of the most powerful early lessons I learned is that when big problems occur, the best strategy is not to call in an army of advisors to sit around and jibber-jabber, but rather to find one or two truly knowledgeable, experienced people who have been through a similar circumstance and can guide, coach, or be truth revealers to the boss. Teams are or may be needed for many things— putting out fires, rebuilding relationships and facilities, reeducating and sometimes rehabilitating employee and community relationships—but as the number of people involved in trying to solve the crucial problem grows, so does the amount of time it takes to get things done. Sometimes situations never get resolved because management fails to bring in the intellect and focus of one or two knowledgeable, trusted strategic individuals. Another lesson is that when recovery missions get muddled, it is the boss who gets fired rather than the advisor or staff people.

The most important step on the way to becoming a trusted strategic advisor is making your personal commitment to becoming one, then publicly and purposefully undertaking the steps and decisions to achieve your goal. Your manifesto, your publicly declared but personal list of daily obligations, is what will set you apart and ensure your success. Talk through these ideas with those you advise; they will be inspired when you do.

The trusted strategic advisor is committed to

- Understanding that leaders think and operate with a focus on solutions; understanding the pressures and obstacles leaders face, what matters from the leader's perspective
- Recognizing and anticipating what leaders expect
- Studying leaders and leadership to understand their patterns of thinking, decision making, and action taking
- Having a relationship with leaders built on trust and service
- Practicing the disciplines of the trusted strategic advisor:

   Being trustworthy

   Becoming a verbal visionary

   Developing a management perspective

   Thinking strategically

   Being a window to tomorrow

   Advising constructively

   Showing the boss how to use your advice

You are on your own (YOYO). Be strategic. Be the table. Solution options are always your responsibility. Find the ingredients of successful strategy. Manage your own destiny by helping leaders achieve theirs.

You can do this. When you do, you will have an important, fulfilling, and happier professional career. See you at the top.

Please let me know what you learn along the way.

James E. Lukaszewski
tlg@e911.com
www.e911.com

Index